When Billows Roll

Adventures with God Through Lyme Disease

Paul Ashley

SeeLight
Publishing
Toney, Alabama

When Billows Roll
Adventures with God Through Lyme Disease

Unless otherwise indicated,

ISBN: 978-0-9894452-2-1

Published by:
SeeLight Publishing
Toney, Alabama

*This book is joyfully dedicated to
anyone who needs a little encouragement
in the storms of life…
and sooner or later, just about everyone.*

Acknowledgements

My wife, Joan, has been a cheerful companion on countless medical excursions, without which the adventures would simply not be the same. She never hesitated to be by my side at every turn, no matter how sharp or steep.

I would like to thank my sister, Beth, for her very helpful research and thoughtful advice in understanding tick-borne diseases as well as the vast array of treatment approaches.

I would also like to thank Stephanie Anderson and Jason Orr of Jera Publishing for their advice and thoughtful help in the book preparation.

FOR WITH THEE IS THE FOUNTAIN OF LIFE;
IN THY LIGHT WE SEE LIGHT.

— PSALMS 36:9

Contents

Preface

According to estimates of the Center for Disease Control there are about 300,000 new cases of Lyme disease in the United States each year, not including other tick borne co-infections. Furthermore, according to The New England Journal of Medicine, an estimated 10-20% of those treated for Lyme will have recurring, often debilitating symptoms. This is sometimes called chronic Lyme disease. Because the tests for Lyme disease are, for a variety of reasons, unreliable and many of the symptoms are clinical, that is, not subject to physical testing, the actual number of cases could be much higher. Also, the other tick-borne co-infections may contribute to the symptoms of the illness as well.

In spite of the increased spread of the disease, the modern medical profession has generally not been able to respond adequately with effective diagnosis or treatment. Modern medicine depends upon physical tests for diagnosis and treatment guidance. Lyme disease has for a long time defied almost all of these tests and is about as deft as Tweety Bird at stringing along Sylvester the cat. Sylvester tried everything he could possibly do and quite a few things he could not do to nab Tweety, making for classic entertainment…affectionately known as *"Looney Tunes"*.

Traditionally, the medical profession for the most part packs just two tools in its tool box, synthetic drugs and a scalpel. If surgery is not warranted, then for the most part, drugs constitute the remaining option. And if drugs do not work, then all that is left is a song and dance. Some of those routines in the doctor's office, by the way, can be almost as amusing as a Warner Bros. cartoon.

Dealing with the symptoms of Lyme disease day after day, while watching your confidence in the lifeline of modern medicine slip away beyond the waves, can be very sobering. It took several years for my smile to return. Not because I found a perfect cure to the illness, but because I began to step back and view the scene from a new perspective. Join me in a comfortable seat as I share it with you. Perhaps this book will return a smile to your face and hope to your heart.

Introduction

Many are the strange chances of the world ...
— J.R.R. TOLKIEN

A s waiting rooms go this one was rather typical. It was a family practice office of which I had been a patient for more years than I can remember. I had not bothered to secure a family doctor until my late 30's. There seemed to be no need since my health history was particularly unremarkable. The nearby medical clinics which were becoming quite prevalent at the time served well enough for an infrequent sinus infection or other minor acute condition.

I never liked going to the doctor. My mother was a nurse and I had learned early in life as a young child that the best way to avoid an unpleasant dose of medicine or worse yet ... the dreaded shot in a most humbling part of the anatomy, was to deny everything. Unfortunately, no matter how chipper I pretended to appear, I knew that when I was obliged to open my mouth for her that my red swollen tonsils would inevitably give me away. Worse still, in those days, long ago, my Mom always had a vial of penicillin waiting in the refrigerator, the kind with the small rubber seal covering the top secured tightly by a metal retainer band. Sitting next to it was a small black plastic container. The inside of the container was shaped to fit the two parts of a glass syringe along with what I remember to this day as a whoppingly large needle. It was already pre-sterilized, conspicuously waiting there in plain sight every time I opened the refrigerator, waiting for the next victim — I mean sick child. The rest I will leave to your imagination. Let's just say that later, when I became a little older and was occasionally escorted to the doctor for a sore throat or other such malady, I was not a happy camper. And I can only suspect that for most of those left behind in the waiting room, to hear my unearthly utterances of resistance, echoing down the hall, it may have raised a few hairs.

But here I was today, not really wanting to be here but going anyway, partly at the prodding of my wife. Although I had not spent much time in this waiting room over the years, the sights and sounds were well studied, a pastime generally more pleasing to me than reading outdated magazines such as *Woman's Day* or *Good Housekeeping*. The moldings, furniture, even the latest scratches on the wall did not escape my glance as the time slowly ticked by.

There was a display cabinet against the wall, tucked away near the corner of the room. On a shelf behind the glass was a well worn antique leather medical hand bag. Beside it were carefully arranged many of the items which once resided inside. I had time to visually study each one and wonder how long it had been since it was last used on a house call. For a brief moment I pondered how much the practice of medicine had changed, or on the other hand how little, depending on the perspective. Behind me was the sound of other patients shuffling in through the front door and the short repeated interchange with the receptionist. Occasionally, the solid door near the corner of the room quickly opened while a technician in scrubs and bright tennis shoes would emerge with file folder in hand to call the name of the next patient. In between these short disturbances, the waiting room was rather quiet this day.

The receptionist called me back to the desk to hand me a clipboard along with instructions to update my file. This always seemed like a useless exercise, considering that nothing had changed, but everything must be reentered. Nothing about the ritual encouraged me to make my perpetually illegible handwriting any more legible as I hurriedly scrolled out my name and address. I filled in the date, April 29, 2009, as if the receptionist did not already know that. It was close to my turn, as the number of patients who arrived there before me had now dwindled.

The technician opened the door once again, called my name, and down the hall I went. First stop was the weigh-in. Nothing new there. I had weighed within about five pounds of this same weight for the past 35 years. No matter, there was still a habitual hint of nervousness in her graceful approach to eyeing the number as soon as it appeared on the digital display. She had definitely mastered the art of not drawing attention to a patient's weight, no matter where it

landed on the scale. And in a motion rivaling the speed of a
humming bird, dodging from a flower, she had the number
recorded in her file as if by such swift action she was ren-
dered innocent of any embarrassing thought. I don't think
it would have made any difference if someone had bottomed
out the scale. She would have found some way to turn it into
a disarming compliment.

Now we walked further down the hall to an examination
room where I waited again. As before, the room was familiar, albeit less space to peruse while occupying the time.
Keeping very calm from the time that I sat down, I took
the pose of a living statue, breathing lightly and not even
moving so much as the muscles attached to my eyeball.
This exercise had now become almost an obsession each
time I was in the doctor's office while waiting for the nurse
to enter the room. She invariably came in like a person on a
mission, to see how high a blood pressure reading she could
record from a patient that day, or at least that's the way it
seemed. And I was just as determined to not be that patient,
although it was often a considerable challenge.

With a certain mixed measure of concern and glee she
strapped on the arm cuff and gave it a good tug. I wondered
for a moment if her previous career had been cinching calves
at the rodeo. Then she pumped up the cuff, her eyes growing
a little larger with each squeeze of the inflating bulb. The
needle on the extra large dial mounted beside us rose higher
and higher. I was convinced of her intentions to rattle me,
but like any stoic statue, I did my best to resist the assault.
Finally, she announced the result with a booming voice loud
enough to be clearly heard in the hallway while writing it in

big numerals on my chart for the doctor to see. Immediately she exited the room once more, leaving me to wait still again.

I could hear muffled tones of Dr. B's voice as he progressed slowly from room to room, now in the room next to mine. Finally, there was a rustle of paper in the tray attached to the outside of the door as the doctor picked up my chart. After a brief few seconds, time enough for him to take a quick glance at my chart, the door opened. With a big smile accompanied by his practiced pleasant voice, he greeted me by name as if we were close friends, even though I had not seen him in at least a year. It was somewhat reassuring, however, that he appeared to remember my name among so many patients even if he did have the advantage of a quick review from my chart beforehand. Having just given the details of why I was here to the nurse, who wrote it all down, I was obliged to repeat it all once again. While listening with one ear, he thumbed through the thin folder containing my very sparse medical history of the past 20 years.

I explained to Dr. B that it is not uncommon to get several tick bites each year since I live in an area surrounded by woods and spend a considerable amount of time outdoors. Generally, I remove the tick, often discovering it just as it begins to itch, and then over the few days following, a small red bump appears, which slowly resolves over the next couple of weeks. But this time there was a more noticeable red streak which projected a few centimeters laterally on either side of the bump. So as a precautionary measure I had decided to have it examined.

Well, Dr. B proceeded to look it over and explained in his usual calming manner that it did not appear to be of particular concern. The prevailing thought was that although infectious diseases can be carried by ticks, this is a very rare occurrence. As a precautionary measure he told me to watch the site and if it did not resolve within two to three weeks, I should get a prescription filled, which he handed to me while he was talking. It was for Doxycycline.

Dr. B proceeded to make a few notes on my chart and then, as was his practice, he pulled a small compact tape recorder from his white lab coat pocket and dictated a short conversation to himself, interjecting a few of his usual quips and patient flattery for me to hear. Not surprisingly, I always enjoyed this part of the visit, a light moment before his quick exit. I often wondered who it might be that would have occasion to listen to these rhetorical monologues. And how different from reality must be these mental images, which they conveyed of me to that unwary listener.

Then with his white coat almost caught on the door latch, he darted down the hall to the next patient. I followed along a few paces behind carrying the prescription in hand, which I folded once neatly and proceeded to bury in my shirt pocket. Around the corner for a quick stop at the desk near the business office cubicle was all that was left to do. Invariably, I never knew whether to sit in the conspicuously placed chair in front of the desk or just lean awkwardly over it while trying to exchange paperwork and signatures. While I was still halting between these two possibilities, the clerk completed her paperwork. After exchanging smiles, it was just a quick jaunt through a couple of doors and I was out of there.

There is a little clay pot on top of my bedroom chest of drawers, among a menagerie of crowded objects. It is decorated with the almost unrecognizable markings of a five year old, along with the carefully handwritten name of my son Stephen, who is now grown. The pot was a Father's Day project from Sunday School. It remains a cherished memento, but being otherwise empty, it eventually became the repository for doctors' appointment cards and unused prescriptions. Well, as you can imagine, that is where the Doxycycline prescription ended up.

The Distant Cloud

Behind the clouds is the sun still shining…
— HENRY WADSWORTH LONGFELLOW

The spring and summer of 2009 were like most others. We made our usual trip to the beach in the Florida panhandle for a week in May and returned from the respite ready for the days ahead. The outdoors were always very enjoyable for me and working outside was not really work. In the south the summers are very hot and humid. Bugs of all kinds proliferate. Keeping in the shade during midday and drinking plenty of fluids is the usual regiment. By the time fall comes I am usually more than ready for the cooler nights and gentle breezes. This fall we had plans to prepare a shelter and paddock for a new horse. As winter approached I spent much of the time clearing a few large sweet gum trees from the area. So I was not surprised in mid-December when after many hours with the chainsaw I had begun to develop a pain in my left shoulder. Actually,

I would have been surprised if I had not developed a pain somewhere after that much labor. Surely I was entitled to some sort of badge of recognition for such a timberman's accomplishment, not to mention wrestling all those roots out of the ground.

I traveled frequently for business and the second week of December found me at a conference preparing for a speaking engagement in Atlanta. The second night there I got a phone call. As soon as I saw the number I recognized that it was my sister. And as she spoke the first few words I knew that there was something wrong. She told me that my mother, then 85 years old, had fallen and broken her hip. During the next few weeks her condition slowly deteriorated resulting from complications following the surgery to repair the break. By the end of the month we realized that my mother would not likely leave the hospital. During the multiple 90 mile drives to visit her we became successively less hopeful of her condition. The holidays were more sober and my shoulder pain seemed to continually linger. Eventually, I had to limit my outdoor activity.

January came and the first week brought a 4-inch snowfall, rather unusual for this part of the country, which generally is quite capable of emptying every grocery shelf of bread and milk within 100 miles at the mere rumor of more than 5 snowflakes. With a very long driveway, about 600 feet of which is in the shade and not easily thawed, I often spent my time moving the car to the end of the driveway in advance rather than scrambling for the last loaf of crumpled whole wheat at the neighborhood quick stop. The problem, of course, was that upon returning home I was faced with walking the dark winding trail through the woods along the driveway at night, trying to hold onto a flashlight with fading batteries. And while also toting numerous other bags, boxes or other assorted items, this soon diminished the charm of the winter wonderland.

After about the third day of slipping, sliding and toting it was either shovel or continue being stranded. So I shoveled. Needless to say, my shoulder was not thrilled at the prospect of so much exercise. So, it didn't take much encouragement to talk me into an appointment to see an orthopedic doctor on the second week of January. Little did I know what this doctor visit and the year 2010 would hold unseen among the still blank calendar pages hanging on the wall of the kitchen, where appointments were always dutifully recorded.

The shoulder specialist that I had come to see was an older doctor with much experience. I had been to a shoulder specialist before for minor issues and so I knew the routine. I expected the prerequisite x-rays. Then there was a bit of poking, soon followed by his articulating of my shoulder as if trying to determine the greatest range of motion on the arm of a Lego figure. All of this without voicing a sound and then finally breaking the silence, he explained his opinion of my condition along with a course of treatment, perhaps some meds and physical therapy. But this occasion was different. What came next was the first in a long series of surprises and mysteries.

Upon completing his examination, the doctor concluded that there was nothing wrong with my shoulder, but he suspected my neck. I can still recall the silent high pitched voice inside my head that said, "My neeeck!" My neck did not hurt at all, so I was quite puzzled. He sent me back for x-rays of the upper spine. When he entered the room the second time, he informed me that I had two bulging discs and a congenital fusion of two other vertebrae to boot, which a later MRI scan would further confirm. Well, what can I say! I had been told that I was sometimes a little stiff-necked.

So, off I went and then back down the hall the next day where I was sent to the spine specialist. By now the pain radiated down the arm and across the back of the shoulder. Without any further examination he recommended…you guessed it, some meds and physical therapy. A visit to a neurologist for a nerve conduction study of my arm was also set up. Well, with my head still spinning on my newly discovered vertebral flaws, I limped out of the office and down the stairs to my car, feeling 20 years older, the power of suggestion.

The nerve conduction test appeared innocuous enough. Then came the needles. They were inserted one after another in the shoulder and hand. Connected to them were wires and it wasn't long before the neurologist was turning big knobs on a large metal box with both hands at once, then probing for electrical signals back and forth until he was satisfied. He made a few very brief remarks that the nerves in my arm were working, but carefully shortening the number of words used as he spoke, like someone texting with a 142-word limit. Then he headed for the door. I had been in enough doctors' offices to know that when they quickly place their hand on the door lever, you had better think fast if you want any more of their time.

While still reeling from the electric shocks in my arm, I staggered to face the door like a person who has just pulled out the darts from a taser gun. But I was still determined to shake my head and clear my mind well enough to voice a question sufficient to stall his departure. Although I gained little additional information as a result of this heroic effort, the success, under the circumstances, in getting him to take his hand off the door for a few more seconds was somewhat satisfying.

The pain in the left arm, now reaching to the wrist and hand, made sleep difficult and compelled me to contort my elbow and cradle my left forearm in my right hand while standing, or to rest it on any convenient object while sitting. I was told that it would be a long healing process of several months for my neck, which still was, ironically, one of the few places free of pain. With my attention diverted by my arm day and night, what was to come over the next short weeks quickly overwhelmed my conscious ability to take it all in.

There was just the hint of a breeze in the air throughout the heights of Mt. Carmel as the prophet Elijah, who was now spent from the long day's excitement, waited for word from his servant. He had sent him repeatedly off to the distant edge of the mountain to gaze from its heights into the western sky as the sun hovered perilously close to the sea. The prophet of the Lord sat down on the ground, and his head sank slowly between his knees. The loyal servant returned again and again. Finally he reported to Elijah what seemed a curious observation,

> " ... Behold, a cloud as small as a man's hand is coming up from the sea ... "
> *(1 Kings 18:44)*

It appeared of little consequence to the servant who held his hand high at arm's length before his face to shade it from the glaring sun. In so doing, the span of his palm with fingers extended provided a convenient measure of the frail cloud's size. It was just a puff, a wisp on the distant horizon, seemingly rising out of the sea. Hardly had the servant spoken, then Elijah's head snapped up and his hurried voice ordered his servant along. Elijah sensed that there was more, and sure enough it was not long before, "the sky grew black with clouds and wind" as a hard rain began to fall.

We are told that the hand of the Lord was upon Elijah as he gained new found energy and raced down the mountain. He did not stop as he reached the valley below. Quickly tying his loose robe up around his waist, he ran the 17 miles to the outer city gate of Jezreel, outpacing even the chariot of the king as the dust, mingled with the fresh rain, splashed from under its wheels.

What a day it had been for this faithful prophet. He had defended the Lord's name, cleared the kingdom of false prophets, and ushered in the close of a three and a half year long drought. Little did he know as he sped along on the victory run toward the king's palace that the waves churning upon the shore and the clouds amassing overhead were only the beginning. By the next day Elijah was running again, but this time running for his life, fearful of the unknown and what may be in pursuit. Over the next 40 days he was plagued with a sense of hopelessness and helplessness. He struggled along, weak from hunger, travelling up to 400 miles of desert roads and then climbed the 7000-foot jagged peak of Mt. Sinai. There Elijah collapsed in a cave as exhaustion closed in around him. How quickly things had changed. And it all started with a small cloud the size of a hand.

> *God moves in a mysterious way*
> *His wonders to perform;*
> *He plants his footsteps in the sea*
> *And rides upon the storm.*
>
> *Ye fearful saints fresh courage take;*
> *The clouds ye so much dread*
> *Are big with mercy and shall break*
> *In blessings on your head.*
> — WILLIAM COWPER,
> *LIGHT SHINING OUT OF DARKNESS*

Complicit Denial

Denial ain't just a river in Egypt.

— MARK TWAIN

Mom's funeral was the first week of February. With my painful arm in tow, I performed the funeral service. It was a small gathering of family members. Although we all missed her very much, we knew her pain was now over and, I could only imagine with joy the new delight she had found with the Lord, whom she was very fond to mention at every possible opportunity for as long as I can remember as a child.

I had many times maneuvered through the familiar doors and hallways on the long walks from the parking garage to her room on the second floor of the hospital. Sitting in a chair by the window near the foot of her bed with my arm carefully adjusted on the side rest, I automatically shifted it back and forth, searching for a comfortable spot while talking to her. My mind was occupied with impending loss. As the strength in her frail body faded over those final weeks, I sensed the departure of a great prayer warrior. A chill came over me at what that loss may mean in the future for each of us in the family. We could not possibly know what unseen support those daily prayers of hers had been to us over the years. But I would be reminded of this passing thought countless times in months, even years, to come.

On the way home from these trips, we would often stop for dinner as the sun set. Each time, I tried to think of an inconspicuous way to ask for a table next to a ledge to rest my left arm. I may have drawn some strange looks, sizing up the height of the ledge beside the potentially suitable table to see if my arm would line up at just the right spot.

The weekend after the funeral brought with it the first of many surprising and mysterious symptoms. It began with the appearance of muscle tremors in the chest. An after-hours doctor on call at the orthopedic center assured me that this was probably related to the neck inflammation. I smiled and politely hung up the phone with the same gestures and facial expressions as if I were standing in front of him in his office, while in reality I was dressed in an old pair of jeans and standing in my bedroom. Isn't it interesting that we accept favorable information from a doctor so quickly, and how easily we sometimes allow him to dispel our concerns. Anyway, I was happy as a lark...for a while.

Well, the respite was short lived. By Monday morning the pain in my left arm had projected sharply down to the hand and there was now a tightness in my right arm, as well as tingling in my legs, feet and hands. My orthopedic doctor, however, was still not at all deterred. After enduring my monologue of the latest episode in my meandering tale, all the while nurturing a serious composure, he hustled me off for an appointment with a physical therapist. But not before interjecting a tale or two of his own personal experiences for good measure in an attempt to make me feel better.

The physical therapy center was located down a long flight of stairs. With the resonating sound of the large metal door closing behind me along with the multiple echoes of the mechanical clanks and shrieks beyond my sight, the word "dungeon" came to mind. But I continued to play along. After all, by now 4 doctors and a chiropractor all agreed that it was all really just a pain in my neck. How could I argue with that, even if I was by now beginning to feel like an electrically charged pin cushion while my neck was just about the only part of my body relatively free of symptoms.

A train of thoughts must have circled through Elijah's mind as he sat in the secluded cave, surrounded by despair. Even as one thought faded into another he listened and, "a great and strong wind was rending the mountains and breaking in pieces the rocks". Then under his feet he felt an earthquake. After the earthquake he felt the heat and saw the flashing brightness of a fire. Then finally, "with the sound of a gentle blowing", there was a very gentle breeze as if the breath of someone speaking. He pulled his mantle up over his face reflexively.

As Elijah stood up and walked to the entrance of the cave, God's comforting voice was heard. Everything that had preceded it emptied him of all expectations. Indeed, it is our expectations that often lead us into the cave of despair and confusion where the "still small voice" is there to reassure us. (1 Kings 19:11,12 KJV)

> *Jesus! what a help in sorrow!*
> *While the billows o'er me roll,*
> *Even when my heart is breaking,*
> *He, my comfort, helps my soul.*
> — JOHN WILBUR CHAPMAN,
> *JESUS! WHAT A FRIEND FOR SINNERS!*

Turning up the Megaphone

The first physical therapy session was physical, although it was anything but therapeutic. I wondered if there was a hidden camera somewhere capturing all of this for a comic TV show. The last time that I had been to an orthopedic doctor, I was given a paper copy of some exercise instructions complete with cartoon figures illustrating the various poses and movements. Then the attendant at the desk reached into a cabinet and pulled out two giant rubber bands, one red and one green. With a few quick tips on how to use the bands without smacking myself in the face, I was sent home as she donned a hopeful smile. Actually I had managed rather well at that time…that is once I remembered that after attaching the rubber band to a door knob, make sure the door is securely closed before grabbing the other end and stretching tightly at arm's length across the chest.

But that was then and this was now. I was ushered into a large room by a therapist dressed in a stylish matching suit of scrubs, blue on blue, along with an equally trend setting pair of tennis shoes. With a bit too much cheer in her voice, she pointed to one of the many chairs lined up on one side of the room and instructed me to hop in. After a few brisk adjustments by the therapist I found myself leaning back precariously. For a second there came over me the same ominous shiver that I get when first staring at the ceiling in a dentist's chair and hearing the rattling of activity out of sight behind me, meant to not be seen.

Next came thermal treatments of the neck and shoulder followed by an electric shock treatment. The attendant strategically placed electrodes on the back of my neck and then turned up the voltage incrementally, periodically asking if I could feel anything. It was not long before my shoulders and arms were quivering to the repetitive beat with each successive pulse, dutifully inflicting its prerequisite dose of sharp pain. However, before I could get the words out during a fleeting half second between pulses, to beg some relief, she vanished into thin air, but not before setting a timer on this malicious beast. I was inescapably trapped by the wires and the recurring shocks.

When the timer sounded and the treatment stopped I was looking for the door. Before I could make my early exit the attendant reappeared out of nowhere. I can only say that it must have been brain fog that keep me from coming up with some excuse quickly enough to take my leave on this occasion. I was ejected from the chair, and while hobbling forward, was taken into another smaller room with no windows.

I knew that I was in trouble upon seeing what looked like a medieval rack prominently placed opposite the door. It did not take long to discover once again the particularly common practice of abandonment in which physical therapists apparently take great delight, and which would add considerably to my trepidation. As a captive patient, I was completely immobilized with harness, wrappings, or electrical connections, and after several adjustments to a little control box which sets into motion a timed sequence of tortuous undulations… the therapist deftly left the room.

For the succeeding 30-40 minutes, through a harness firmly attached under my jaw, this animated machine tugged repeatedly on my spine. With renewed glee, on each cycle it stretched, ratcheting little by little, as if listening to hear if it had yet succeeded in dislodging a vertebrae or two. I was ready to confess anything the therapist wanted to know when she finally returned. Apparently oblivious to my frozen countenance and exhausted eyes, she calmly assured me that it might take several sessions to notice an improvement. She tried to further console me by relating her own personal story of a painful experience with a compressed nerve in her neck. With my neck about half an inch longer and my arms and legs twitching, however, her calm voice and storytelling was of no comfort. Meanwhile, I quietly assured myself that like a frightened cat, I would soon put as much distance between me and this machine as my legs would serve to propel me.

As I breezed by the checkout counter where I was asked about scheduling my next appointment, I mumbled something about getting back with them later. I made my way out to the parking lot, gasping as if having just emerged from several minutes at the bottom of a swimming pool. Well, at least now I could say that my neck was no longer pain free.

If this was not enough, I was given a prescription for a portable neck stretching device to use in my leisure time at home. I don't know if it was curiosity or dullness of the mind that led me down the street to the store front of a small medical supply to which I had been directed. The attendant took my prescription and disappeared for a brief moment through the door beside her. She returned with an inconspicuous box and set it on the counter. Expecting that I would need some instruction on its use, she opened the box and revealed a contraption with a large collar composed of various plastic and rubber materials. Dangling hypnotically from one side was a rubber squeeze bulb.

As she then demonstrated, the idea was to tightly strap the collar around the neck, just shy of strangulation, and then inflate the bladder inside the collar with the hand pump to apply pressure between the shoulder and the base of the skull. All of this while interjecting a story about a cousin twice removed who had a similar problem and this procedure, once a day, worked wonders … or something like that.

I managed to unpack it that night to try out on my sore neck from the therapy session. Sitting down in a comfortable chair, I strapped on the collar and started pumping. A few seconds later it felt like an over inflated tire inner tube around my neck. I was not sure which was going to burst first, the collar or my bulging eyeballs. In the meanwhile the downward pressure introduced pain on my shoulders in new places. I cut the 20 minute session short and with my last bit of strength and sanity, I managed to reach the air relief valve to deflate this sadistic invention. I put it back in the box and sealed it up, hoping that I would not have nightmares of it escaping to torment me again, as I placed it high on a shelf in the hall closet.

Sitting in front of the TV one evening I thought I heard a barely audible high pitched tone. My first thought was that it may have come from the TV set. Having worked with electronics most of my life, I was quite familiar with tones of this type and of similar frequency, which are sometimes generated by the signal which controls the screen display. On older TV sets these annoying tones could be quite noticeable, particularly for those who were young enough to still have good sensitivity at high pitch. Not that I was that young any more. Even so, wishfully wanting to think otherwise, I continued my effort to convince myself that it was nothing more. Try as I might, I soon had to admit that it was primarily my left ear and could not be attributed to the TV at all.

It did not take me long to check it out further. With a bit of research I discovered that such sounds in the ear, called tinnitus, were listed as one of the possible side effects of the drug that I had been given by the orthopedic doctor a few weeks before to relieve my nerve pain. I immediately stopped taking it since it was not helping at all anyway. And I fully expected the tinnitus to soon resolve. Little did I realize at the time that this particular symptom would linger with me from then on and only steadily grow worse over the course of the next year. It was the first of what was soon to be many unrecognized signs that there was more going on than a pain from the neck.

This persistent tone in the ear chased me like a kamikaze mosquito, day and night. I tugged and stretched and wiggled my ear lobe incessantly. I twitched and leaned my head repeatedly to the left, as if hoping something would fall out. I wrung my jaw from side to side and gnawed the air. I invented every acrobatic maneuver that one could imagine using every muscle surrounding my skull. All was to no avail. The only result was a red, swollen ear and an occasional twitch on that side of the face. The tinnitus had become an ever present emblem of the elusive enigma, which was soon to unfold.

The prophet Isaiah brought God's words of comfort and assurance to the people of Israel.

When you pass through the waters, I will
be with you;

And through the rivers, they will not
overflow you...
(Isaiah 43:2)

God promised to be with them, and because of this they
would not be overcome as their trials billowed. Though
the waves rise high and the current runs swift, God's presence is never lacking. Just the same, all true children of
God may find comfort here as sure as that promised to the
Israelites long ago. The malady of an elusive condition such
as Lyme disease may billow from day to day and month to
month. But each wave with its sense of greater peril serves
to heighten our sense of an ever present, watchful God.
Psalms 66, probably written by King David, suggests our
response to such a thought.

Bless our God, O peoples,
And sound His praise abroad,
Who keeps us in life
And does not allow our feet to slip.
For You have tried us, O God;
You have refined us as silver is refined.
(Psalms 66:8-10)

The phrase translated, "Who keeps us in life", is literally
in the Hebrew, "Puts our soul in life". The Lord keeps our
feet from slipping as He uses the relentless, uncertain trials
to refine us as pure silver. And in doing so He places our
soul in life. He gives life to our soul. True life is in harmony

with God. It is focused on God. And for most of us that can take a lot of refinement.

There are few trials quite like a chronic condition such as Lyme or its related infections, which rattle your vital organs. And all the while it leaves you with a sense of abandonment as you realize that there is no real medical understanding of your condition. This sense of abandonment increases as each medical approach and each doctor reaches a dead end. The doctors are ultimately without words or wisdom. They have no answers. You discover that they were not taught about this condition in medical school. They cannot tell you if you will get better or worse. They cannot even tell you if you will live or die. They just don't know. They have no past observations or future prognosis. This process repeats itself over and over with each medical pursuit. The higher the expectation, the deeper is the abandonment which follows because you know the list of new possibilities for answers is now growing very slim. The psalm continues,

> ... We went through fire and through water,
> Yet You brought us out into a place of abundance.
> *(Psalm 66:12)*

For the Israelites, the fire and water represented a seemingly endless journey through a lonely wilderness. But the psalmist realized that God was with them all along the way. And they could only fully appreciate the place of abundance against the backdrop of their trials. So it is with us. How much more may we appreciate the abundance of our soul placed in life, purified as silver, keen to His presence all along the way.

> *God brings men into deep waters not to drown them, but to cleanse them.*
> — James H. Aughey

Unsettling Doubt

There was a castle called Doubting Castle, the owner whereof was Giant Despair.

— JOHN BUNYAN

My next visit to the doctor came at the beginning of March. By this time I realized that I needed to carry a list with me to keep track of the growing symptoms and their many perturbations. The orthopedic doctor now greeted me as if I were a regular patient ... which by now I was. And he could see that I was worn down enough to consider the "dreaded" epidural steroid treatment. This involved an outpatient visit to the hospital where a very looooong needle was inserted from the back of my neck into my spine under general anesthetic. Need I say more?

During the interim week since my last visit the tingling had become stronger and progressed to a burning pain in the hands and feet. There were times when I felt weak-kneed. It was difficult to stand for any length of time and my legs felt like those of a grasshopper who couldn't hop. They just wobbled down the hallway on their own at the office. I was so overcome with shivers throughout the chest in the middle of the night that it precipitated another call to the doctor. But once again, it turned out to be a fruitless attempt to unearth any reasonable explanation for the growing invasion in my body.

I made my way to the hospital appointment for the epidural, soon to find myself in a flimsy gown lying on a gurney. Looking to either side I was not alone. The numerous other patients, separated by thin curtains, one by one carried on conversations with the doctor as they were prepared to be ushered into the procedure. I am sure that I am not the first one who passed the time by eavesdropping with tilted ear on these short vignettes. So when I saw the curtain in front of me suddenly pulled aside with the raking sound of the metal curtain hangers on the rail above, as if the rattle of keys in a jail cell, I was ready. I had my own conversation well rehearsed even before the doctor made his appearance.

Although I had not met this doctor before, since he was the specialist performing only this procedure, I quickly abbreviated the niceties, while calculating to secure a few more seconds of his time to discuss my concerns. Nevertheless, I was surprisingly set back by the bluntness of his response to my condition. Upon enumerating the symptoms in my arm and elsewhere, I emphasized the lack of pain in the neck and gestured with my hand accordingly.

Then I paused hoping for some insight from his copious experience, as evidenced by the chain of patients which he attended to with this procedure each day. He nodded emotionlessly, and simply said in a mostly unmodulated voice that his procedure will probably not help with those symptoms. Then without pausing for my reaction, he proceeded to make a few notes as he slipped between the folds of the curtain, in wait for me to be wheeled down the hall to the operating room.

Moments later I was rolling along, pulled by one attendant at the front, pushed by another at the rear and steered at times by both, mercilessly dodging pedestrians at a fast pace. Fading from view behind me were the curtained cubicles in the distance. I could imagine the patients they contained, who if they had been in earshot of my conversation with the doctor, must surely be hoping for themselves a little better prognosis than mine upon his return to see them off. Meanwhile the doctor's words were still circling in my brain like a stuck vinyl record, complete with the staccato click of the phonograph needle as it skipped over and over — "probably not help, *click*, probably not help, *click*, probably not …".

The procedure did not last long, which is easy to say, considering that I slept through most of it. Since my expectations were very low by this time, it was at least hard to be disappointed when I experienced no improvement within the next few days. The nerves in my hands and body had become jittery along with pins and needles and muscle tightness. I went to see Dr. B at the end of the week, at least just to report in like a good soldier. The focus remained on the elusive "neck problem" although credibility for this tiresome explanation was now, for me, becoming very strained.

A truck load of lumber recently delivered behind the house beckoned me. I had always spent a lot of time working outdoors. In spite of the pain in my shoulder and arm, I was determined to complete this project to build a paddock in preparation for the horse that was soon to arrive. The post holes for the wooden fence had been dug back in blissful December. It was this activity which was accepted by my orthopedic doctor as a plausible if not satisfying explanation for the neck inflammation, at least as far as he was concerned. Most of the posthole digging was done with an auger implement attached to the back of my tractor. It required the constant twisting of my neck and torso all the way around to the rear while one arm remained forward to manage the controls. My body was like a torsion pendulum clock, winding up, back and forth.

In addition, some of the more rocky areas demanded a lot of brutal hand work to chip past large stone. One large boulder had gotten the best of me, as the large gaping crater near the new horse shelter would attest. It was a testament to my persistence in trying to unearth the boulder which lay square in the location of the very last post. Exhausted, I stood with hands on hips, at the crater's edge, piles of dirt high on every side. There the boulder remained, rising from the floor of the crater like an excavated monolith from ancient times. Maybe I could erect a plaque and give tours ... But no. Eventually I engaged the services of a backhoe to win the final victory.

Nonetheless, I was ready to install the fence — however, my arm was not. With the help of a neighbor and some time spent in training my youngest son to successfully drive a nail until he was sufficiently proficient, the fence soon stood tall. I was thankful at the outcome, but wondered if the sharp pain that projected through the center of my hand and exited in the web of flesh between two fingers would ever resolve.

Still another week passed as the stinging hands and feet worsened and to that was added tremors and shivers that lasted much of the night. That week ended with another visit to the orthopedic doctor on Friday, who had been treating my neck. My list of symptoms was growing and intensifying. I was glad to get a last minute appointment even if it was at 7:30 am. And I am not a morning person.

It was a chilly morning and I waited uneasily in the exam room, shivering mildly as I studied the pictures on the wall to pass the time. By now I found it expedient to carry a folder with my notes to each doctor visit. It wasn't long before the door opened and the doctor stepped in. I began to recite the list, my eyes occasionally dropping to check my notes and pausing on occasion to dramatize with hand gestures or facial expressions.

The doctor listened for a while without comment until I began to describe a tightness in the scalp above the eyes and nerve sensations in the side of the head, motioning vividly with my hands behind my ears. Suddenly he stopped me and said matter-of-factly, "This isn't your neck!" "It is something systemic," he continued. It was as if the light had finally come on ... at least partly. I could sense it in his tone of voice. He instructed that I go back to my family doctor and have him review the symptoms again with this in mind.

I was determined to survive until Monday morning, if for nothing else than to approach Dr. B with this new found authority that there was really something else wrong. But making it over the weekend would turn out to be a challenge. In addition to an intensification of all the other symptoms, a completely new one was added to the list. I began to have chest spasms which caused heart palpitations and coughing.

How does one measure patience? For some it is seconds or hours. For those with a condition like Lyme it is generally months or years. Perhaps one of the most difficult Godly attributes to master is patience. But what desperate souls we would be if God were not the master of patience Himself.

The Apostle Peter was definitely not known for his patience. He once drew a knife and cut off the ear of the high priest's official when they came for Jesus. His faith grew and he learned to use it to place his trust in the Lord. Near the end of his life's ministry Peter wrote two letters to Christian believers, which are recorded in the Bible. At the beginning of the first letter he instructed them that their

faith would be tested. And the trial itself would prove their
faith's worth.

> That the trial of your faith, being much more
> precious than of gold that perisheth ...
> *(1Peter 1:7)*

In his second letter Peter explained this more fully, based
on the many experiences of his ministry, the persecution
of fellow believers, and his own imminent martyrdom. He
wrote with the earnestness and urgency of someone who
had exhaustedly traveled a long road and wanted to pass
along sure directions to others. He said that faith is just
the beginning in a rewarding path that leads toward the
knowledge and glory of God. With diligence, he urged that
faith not be the end in itself.

> And beside this, giving all diligence, add to your
> faith virtue ...
> *(2 Peter 1:5, KJV)*

The word translated, "add", is the Greek verb *epichorégeó*
from which we get the word, "chorus". It means to richly
supply as for a grand performance. The verb is in the aorist
tense and imperative mood. This indicates that the action
or admonition is to be carried out to completion. We are
to use our faith as a supply to create a grand performance
of our lives for God. Peter then lists seven specific attributes to which we should attain. The first is virtue or moral
excellence. Interestingly, the fifth is translated "patience" in

the KJV Bible. It is the Greek word, *hupomoné*, taken from two words, one which means "under" and the other means "remain", or when put together, "remaining under", "endurance", steadfastness". God given faith allows the believer to remain under, endure the challenges He allots to us in life. By doing so, we become a part of the grand performance of God's work in this world.

> *Never be afraid to trust an unknown future to a known God.*
>
> — Corrie ten Boom

Much Advice, Little Comfort

The only thing to do with good advice is to pass it on. It is never of any use to oneself.

— OSCAR WILDE

hortly after dawn arrived on Monday morning, I left a message with Dr. B and headed for the emergency room. He called back to my cell phone while I was on my way and urged me to come to his office instead. He knew me well enough to believe that I was not in life-threatening danger at the time. He convinced me that there would be no help for me at the emergency room, admitting that they would be just as useless as other doctors had been so far. There was a certain desperation in his argument.

I adjusted my course and headed to his office. He got me right in and I explained what the orthopedic doctor had told me. He listened attentively until I had finished. There was a bit of uncertainty, then a hint of puzzlement. I could see the gears turning, albeit slow at first. It was as if he was waiting for all of my symptoms to somehow line up as members in a choir. He seemed to be listening for the sound of some harmony in it all. But I could tell from his posture and the expression on his face that whatever sound he was hearing was not the Brooklyn Tabernacle Choir, for sure. No, I've seen that face before, listening to a choir. I think it was in the small town of Mayberry.

Then, not to be outdone, he did something that only Dr. B would do. He got up, excused himself with a low tone in his voice, and left the room for a brief moment. When he returned there was in his hand a small well worn paperback volume. He sat down on a little round stool near the door. The height adjustment was very low and his long legs lifted his knees above the level of the seat. He leaned back slightly until his shoulders almost rested against the wall as he opened the book with an inquisitive look. I could not see the title but it soon became clear that it was a compact medical handbook.

Shuffling confidently through the pages he settled on a place where he began to read aloud. It then became obvious that it was a list of possible causes for nerve symptoms similar to mine. One by one he would look up, holding his place in the book with one finger, think for a second, and then say, "No, that's not your problem." or, "You are not a candidate for that." He ended with a few mental notes of things to test as his mouth tightened and curled slightly to one side.

Flipping briskly through my chart he found my insurance information. Then satisfied with what he read, he proceeded to speak aloud while writing notes. And with that the tests began. This included blood tests, a second MRI of the brain, and a heart monitor for starters. This was the first mention of a Lyme test, buried at the bottom of the list of blood tests and he made little to-do about it. But it was only the standard Elisa test, known to be more statistically inaccurate than accurate and not even recommended by the CDC once a patient was symptomatic. Neither I nor Dr. B realized that at the time. In fact all I knew about Lyme was the little that I had recently read while scanning over all the possibilities on the internet for my sudden barrage of symptoms.

As Dr. B and I parted from his office that day, we both thought that we were on the verge of a great discovery, and the mystery would soon be revealed. But in hindsight it was more like the last scene with Indiana Jones in *Raiders of the Lost Ark*. The long sought for prize, hidden in a nondescript wooden crate was carried into a huge warehouse. There it was deposited among endless rows and stacks of other unidentifiable crates of all sizes and shapes, stretching out as far as the eye could see. Well, unaware of the daunting task ahead, it was as if I was now about to open that warehouse door....

The early blood tests came back the next day, showing only a slight deficiency in B12 but not enough to explain my problem. Dr. B may not have been waiting with bated breath on the rest of the test results to come in, but by this time I certainly was, as the next few days dragged on. The continued increase in chest spasms and heart palpitations drove me to an after-hours call one evening eventually answered by an associate of Dr. B instead. Bordering on a patronizing tone she clearly voiced her opinion that Lyme was an extremely unlikely cause and placed her confidence in the B12, for which I was now receiving shots. She said, "There is no Lyme disease in North Alabama." Her strong opinion prompted me to feel better for just about 5 minutes after hanging up the phone. By that time sanity had returned and my confidence in doctors' opinions was sinking fast.

A couple of days later the Lyme test results were back. The doctor's office did not think it significant enough to contact me. Upon inquiring, I discovered that it was negative. I was resigned to accept the result without question, having no idea at the time of how useless the test really was. And I also had no idea how many times in the next few months and years that I would hear the exact same quote down to the word, *"There is no Lyme disease in North Alabama."* It was as if every doctor had read this in the same medical school textbook. And with such conviction, I assume that they all thought that they had gotten this question right on their exam. Well, if doctors could wish it so, I suppose the ticks in North Alabama must be quite healthy... no Lyme disease allowed.

In the meantime, Dr. B had scheduled me to see the neurologist again. My symptoms were increasing so rapidly, that he thought the progression warranted a second look. "Maybe something had changed within the past two months," he pondered, with a hint of puzzlement in his voice. I will have to say, it seemed more like going in a circle to me.

The next day I located the neurologist's office building and proceeded to the 4th floor. It was a small waiting room. Scattered along a few bare places on the wall were tacked some posters, each portraying a scary neurological disease or disorder. My mind began to wander. I thought of all the many such posters and diagrams that I had viewed, decorating doctors' offices and exam rooms, which rapidly returned to my memory from the past. I wondered what the point was of providing the patient with so many possible ailments to choose from as they pondered the mysterious cause of their own problems. They were only to become a nervous wreck even before the neurologist stepped in.

After a number of the usual finger movement and tiptoe exercises, the doctor concluded his exam on me. The conclusion … it's the B12 deficiency. "Just give it time", he said as he made his usual masterfully quick exit, this time with a young medical student in tow. Following just behind them as they went, I stretched to prod him with one more question before he escaped into the long hallway. After all I had seen news reporters do this all the time, chasing uncooperative celebrities with embarrassing questions as they accelerated their pace. The only thing missing was a microphone in my hand and a man trailing behind, balancing a camera on his shoulder as he was about to trip trying to keep up. I asked the doctor about the frequent nerve shocks which spontaneously ran up the sides of my head, jolting my brain and often preventing sleep. He didn't break his stride, but only turned to the student who was stepping fast to stay aside him. He explained mostly for the student's benefit that this is to be expected with B12 deficiency, and would resolve with time over several months or more. I could see that the student dutifully took all this in, but every time I remember that scene now, it always brings a smile.

Dr. B had begun to sense my frustration. He didn't hesitate when I asked to see another orthopedic doctor for a second opinion about the neck and whether the bulging vertebrae could possibly be the cause of so much turmoil in my body. So he scheduled an appointment.

Well, the short answer to my question from this additional doctor was no. There was not likely a connection. But sitting quietly after reviewing a new set of my x-rays, this seasoned orthopedic surgeon let me know that he would be glad to do more tests. He began to describe inserting a probe in a vein in my leg and proceeding up from there. That was enough to hear, and I politely declined. To this day I am not sure it was a serious recommendation or a cleaver ploy to send me scrambling away for his own amusement. In either case, it worked. I was still just trying to get over shivering at the thought of the epidural that I had recently suffered through.

So, I was back to Dr. B at 9:45 am the next morning to report in. I am sure by this time he was not so happy to see me when he viewed his patient appointment list for the day. But he was a trooper. The last time I had been in to see him, he wrote me a prescription for a sedative. And I am sure that he knew soon into this visit that the sedative was not going to be the solution to my problem ... or to his. My symptoms were still on high volume and I explained that the latest orthopedic doctor was not inclined to associate these symptoms with my neck.

He rambled for a short while and then began to tell me about his mother. Many years ago she suffered from nerve pains in her extremities. He related how he and others had tried to find the cause, but eventually it was diagnosed as "idiopathic" neuropathy. This was the first appearance of this term in any of my conversations with him or other doctors. It is derived from two Greek words, *idios*, which means of "one's own", and *pathos*, which means "suffering", or a disease of its own kind, without a known cause. Interestingly, the word *idiotes* from which we get the English word "idiot" comes from this same Greek word. Hard as I try, I cannot for the life of me help but think of that when I hear the term "idiopathic" used ...

Have you ever wondered uneasily if the person in front of you could read your mind and know what you were thinking? Well, if ever I fearfully thought this might be true, it was in the next few moments. Dr. B looked at me and although he did not appear to break his stride in the conversation, the subject suddenly changed. I had always known him to be one of the most compassionate doctors I had ever met. Perhaps it was the strain of so many office visits over such a short time and so little progress, actually no progress, only mounting frustration. He rested his hands down on his chair and said, "Doctors are really just technicians."

He let that sink in for a while as if just revealing a great fearful secret.

Then he explained with a sigh that the modern medical practice is great if you have a broken bone or diabetes or some other such condition, but can be virtually useless with anything that doesn't fit within these limited confines. Although it was a deflating response to hear at that moment, it was at the same time perhaps the most refreshing thing that I had heard a doctor say. In the midst of all the stress, it brought a strange sense of relief. The conflict of trying to convince the doctor was at once removed. There was little more that he could offer, but I knew that he was there for me.

It was now the end of March. The journal that I had started in January consisted of black and white printed pages, copied from a calendar. The daily dated boxes were each increasingly annotated. The entire page for the month of March was completely filled, every space, with print so fine that I strained to read it. It required me to maintain a repeatedly sharpened pencil if it was ever to be legible.

Although Dr. B reassured me that he really did not believe that there was anything wrong with my heart, he recommended that I follow up on an appointment that he had made with the heart center to check it out anyway. I could tell now that his actions had begun to be conspicuously couched in the notion that he was checking things off of a list, more for my sake than his. But he made a point of encouraging me with the explanation that the cardiologist was an internist by training and might offer a fresh perspective on the unrelenting mystery.

I was just thankful daily if I could get out of bed and make it through the day amid tremors, chills, lightheadedness, nerve jerks, stinging hands and feet, along with the ever present waxing and waning of heart palpitations or chest spasms. Eating was a chore and needed to be finished by about 5:00 pm before the symptoms made it impossible to relax.

The first week of April found me climbing the wide staircase inside the large lofted foyer of the heart center. When the cardiologist walked into the exam room, which was decorated with a few pieces of cardiac measurement equipment, I prepared to keep him focused as well as possible on my larger array of symptoms and related questions. I really was not interested in getting side tracked with a bunch of what appeared to be useless cardiac tests. So without hesitation I proceeded to quickly repeat the comments that Dr. B had made about his inherent skilled training in internal medicine, hoping that a bit of flattery would help. Then I recited again the list of symptoms which he had just then quickly passed over while reading my chart as I was speaking.

Taken off guard by my approach, he shifted his facial expression and suggested that such symptoms may be due to a toxin or infection, spoken as if recalling it from the far back reaches of his mind in medical school training rather than actual experience. But rote or not, those words would be stored away to repeat many times to other doctors in the future in an effort to "turn the light on". And then walking down those same stairs, I promptly dismissed the recommended cardiac tests and relegated them down to the bottom of my list of things to do.

The Bible tells the story of a man named Job, who lived in ancient times. Without warning Job's health suddenly failed. He found himself suffering at the edge of the city, consumed by sores and pain. Although the reader is made aware of God's control and direction throughout this tragic part of Job's life, the story continues from Job's perspective. Most of the content of the 42 chapters consists of a strained dialog between Job and a few of his acquaintances. In their failed attempt to comfort Job they offered long-winded advice, explanations of his condition, and counsel for his recovery. All of it Job eventually found quite futile and objectionable. Having listened to several of them for a while, Job expressed his exasperation,

> ... You are all worthless physicians.
> O that you would be completely silent,
> And that it would become your wisdom!
> *(Job 13:4,5)*

Undeterred, they continued to advance their counsel. Job interrupted,

> Sorry comforters are you all.
> *(Job 16:2)*

Later Job questioned rhetorically,

> How then will you vainly comfort me,
> For your answers remain full of falsehood?
> *(Job 21:34)*

In the midst of an illness, we often turn to the medical profession for help and comfort, resting in the assurance that there are those who may be knowledgeable and helpful. However, with a chronic condition such as Lyme disease, we may find ourselves like Job, at the edge of the city, enduring seemingly hopeless difficulties while disillusioned with the inability of others to help.

The Hebrew word translated physicians in verse 4 is actually a verb in participle form. It comes from the word, *rapha*, which means "to heal" or "to repair". Physicians are supposed to be the healing ones. How discouraging it can be when we come to realize that doctors appear worthless. They cannot heal or repair such conditions. And their words of advice or comfort seem vain (literally, empty words). Job described their actions.

They make night into day, saying,

> "The light is near," in the presence of darkness.
> *(Job 17:12)*

Job's comforters offered false and unrealistic encouragement. Ignorance of chronic illnesses often leads to palliating its symptoms. It is a flickering light that soon fades back into darkness. Job lamented,

> My days are past, my plans are torn apart,
> Even the wishes of my heart.
> Where now is my hope?
> And who regards my hope?
> *(Job 17:11,15)*

Outlook on life is now totally different. Thoughts, actions, management of time, future plans, everything is in a new context. But beyond these changes is the uncertainty and unknown, causing even greater unsettlement of the soul. From Job's perspective, he did not know for sure what his condition was or what precipitated it. He did not know if he would survive, or even if he wanted to. There was no help from anyone around him. And any help could at best be uncertain with an untold number of unanswered questions. How could there be any hope? The last part of verse 15 is literally in the Hebrew, "and my hope, who can see it?" Chronic Lyme disease can bring you to this same point of resignation.

Job's thoughts swing from these depths of despair to the height of expectation as he considers his hope in the Lord.

> Oh that my words were written!
> Oh that they were inscribed in a book!
> That with an iron stylus and lead
> They were engraved in the rock forever!
> As for me, I know that my Redeemer lives,
> And at the last He will take His stand on
> the earth.
> Even after my skin is destroyed,

Yet from my flesh I shall see God;
Whom I myself shall behold,
And whom my eyes will see and not another.
My heart faints within me!
(Job 19:23-27)

He clung to an unseen God, knowing that he would someday see Him. Job wrote a message for the world to read. It was an expression of his commitment to God. His life may be changed. His plans for the future may be changed. Regardless of the outcome, one thing would not change. He would someday be rejoined with the God who seemed so far away at this moment. When we face those times that leave us without understanding, our refuge may be found by inscribing in stone the conviction of our heart toward God.

That is what God honors. Through Job's trials, the Lord taught him. Job came to recognize God's sovereignty. And through it, in ways that he may have been unaware, God's hand remained sure. In the end God used this turn of events in Job's life to increase His blessing upon him.

The LORD blessed the latter days of Job more
than his beginning ...
(Job 42:12)

Even Lyme disease may be used by God to increase His blessing on us. So when our "heart faints" within us, let it be at the thought of the Lord.

The readiest way to escape from our sufferings is, to be willing they should endure as long as God pleases.

— JOHN WESLEY

Nowhere to Hide

"But I don't want to go among mad people," Alice remarked ...

— LEWIS CARROLL

Work in my office had become a considerable challenge over the past 3 months. The pain in the shoulder and arm were beginning to slowly subside. But left in its wake was a menagerie of other ailments. Lack of sleep and constant nerve symptoms made each day difficult. One day I happened to be conversing with a colleague, and I mentioned some of the symptoms that I was having. He related that he also experienced some of these heart related symptoms and nerve stimulation as a result of a thyroid abnormality. By now I was grasping at every lead, so I wasted no time in bringing this to the attention of Dr. B. He was less impressed that my problem was thyroid related or any kind of endocrine related cause since my blood tests were normal. He knew the endocrinologist spoken of by my colleague, but only with considerable vexation, did he consent to call him and persuade him to see me on relatively short notice.

The endocrinologist listened patiently as he looked over my previous blood tests and my unashamed plea for him to think outside of the box. I am not sure if it was just compassion or true interest, but he ordered some more blood tests and scheduled a sonogram. I could tell that he considered it a long shot to find anything. And he didn't. One more dead end lead. I recall that this was the point when I first began to feel that whatever was wrong with me was so out of control and beyond any treatment that I might not survive the continued onslaught. But I put those thoughts out of my mind for a while.

I was soon off on a business trip to Seattle. I had determined to just keep plodding along. I got a rental car and found my hotel. The next morning I picked up a co-worker and we headed to the meeting. I found a parking space in the crowded lot on the far back side of the large building. As I got out and tried to keep pace while we walked to the entrance, I could tell that I was unusually weak. It was a strain just sitting all day and I was glad that I had succeeded in making it through the two days of meetings. I thought again that this cannot continue. I only seem to be worse, but without any medical answers or even recognition from doctors that there was anything wrong.

Day by day the blank spaces on my April calendar filled with the same word descriptions. Near the end of the

month there was a date marked to return to the orthopedic doctor. This was the first time to see him since
he had ignited the search for something other than an
orthopedic cause of my problem. I brought him up to date
on the many unsuccessful trails that had been explored.
Determined to not give up yet, I questioned him about the
possibility that my chest spasms and related symptoms in
my throat may somehow be related to pressure from the
bulging vertebrae. I also mentioned a new term that I had
learned, "esophageal spasm". He walked out to retrieve my
X-rays and looked them over again with a long "hmm".
Then he turned full circle to the assistant at the desk and
took this as a great opportunity to send me off with an
appointment to a gastrointestinal doctor that he knew. All
the while, I could not help but think that he was hoping I
would not soon return.

A couple of days later, I met the GI doctor. He listened
to my list of symptoms, as I had them well rehearsed by
now, having chosen just the right adjectives to poignantly
describe each one. Paying little heed, he ordered a few tests
as doctors like to do. I drew the line when he came to one in
which he described with a bit too much pleasure, a sensor
placed down the throat to the stomach for an extended
period of time. When all the tests results returned normal,
and he was pressed for a conclusion, he searched for a diag-
nostic that would seem appropriate to the portion of the
clinical symptoms that I had described which related most
closely to his specialty, and then dismissed the others without a word. "Acid reflux could cause your problem," he said.
Suddenly he appeared to be totally satisfied and content.

And with that brief pronouncement his diagnosis was complete, along with another prescription.

Since January I had now accumulated innumerable prescriptions in this same manner. So I had gathered them up and began to place them in a gallon sized ziplock bag. One by one as I filled a prescription, tried it for a few days or weeks and found it to be useless, I tossed it in. By now the bag was mostly full and this most recent prescription ended up there as well.

It was now the first week of May. And as was our custom for many years now, our annual trip to Florida had been in the planning for some time. I will admit that I am a creature of habit, so packing the car and turning south down the highway was almost like being on autopilot. Upon arrival at the beach house and unloading the car we begin to relax. But that was the problem. My body would not, could not relax. Nerves that I did not know I had were excited. Muscles were jittery. The time there and thoughts that passed became milestone memories, as if preserved by a tape recorder and able to be played back any time years later. They were registered like an unwritten journal but just as indelible, perhaps more so. Among these thoughts I was wondering if it would ever end or only grow worse, for I had come to learn during the preceding months that it was not prone to remain the same.

Upon returning from Florida I decided to focus on investigating some symptoms that seemed most prominent and somewhat quantitative, at least I thought so at the time.

I soon found that my analytic bent was not necessarily appreciated.

I located an ENT doctor and had already made an appointment for the Monday morning when I was back in town. It was a tight schedule since I had an afternoon flight for a business trip. He was friendly enough ... for a while. And his tests were not too daunting. I hit him with my symptoms. The tinnitus was nearly constant in the left ear, and the throat spasms were severe enough to cause me to cough repeatedly. He gave me a hearing test and a short endoscopic exam of the throat. Although he did try to rationalize a few possibilities, nothing really made sense. I left straight from his office to the airport, considerably disappointed.

It was only after several more visits to this doctor I would learn that the term "tinnitus" was considered an unmentionable word, another one of those "idiopathic" strains of dark medical aversion. He hid his feelings quite well. But after enduring my engineering-esque description of the tone in my ear, a nearly single frequency at about 10,000 Hertz and a sound level of up to about 70 decibels, he finally broke down. His voice shifted to a more resigned timbre as he admitted that he did not really believe there was likely to be found any known cause or cure for tinnitus and that my appeal in this regard was hopeless.

Eventually, near the end of the same year I was passed off to one outlier doctor in the same group who dared to utter the word "tinnitus" without cringing. He was more than happy to do ear surgery after subsequently diagnosing me with Meniere's disease. He elucidated that it only required cutting a hole in the side of my head just behind the ear and removing a modest chuck of bone. Needless to say I politely decided to wait on that one. Later he prescribed a steroid inhaler instead, which soon gave me a sinus infection. Into the zip lock bag it went. But I am getting ahead of myself.

Leaving the ENT office, the next three days were spent in Washington DC. I was not feeling well. The nerve shocks in the head were very distracting as I found my way downtown to my hotel. It was a small room with only a view of a rooftop and another building. I lay down to sleep but the nerves in my head would not subside. The next morning I wobbled the three or four blocks to the meeting with an ache in my chest when I breathed. Mentally reviewing the list of doctors and possible causes of my symptoms, I revisited the cardiac tests that I had indefinitely postponed. I almost wished there was something wrong with my heart. At least it would bring the uncertainty to an end.

At the first break I dug up the phone number for the heart center and scheduled an appointment. The earliest date was 4 weeks away. Somehow I knew it would turn up nothing. And when the time did come I was given a glowing report. The routine at the heart center included a complete workup. I endured it all, the treadmills, sonograms and radioimaging, without much incentive to really explain my lengthy list of ailments as I had before. I was exhausted with the effort and just listened indifferently as the technicians found everything normal.

King David spent much of his life fleeing or hiding, in conflict with people who were around him. When he was a boy, he was an object of ridicule by his older brothers. Toward the end of his life, he was a fugitive from his own family when his son Absalom conspired against him. But most notably, from the time of his youth he lived under the relentless persecution of King Saul until the king's sudden death in a battle with the Philistines.

Backed by the armies of Israel and the power of the throne, King Saul was an ever oppressive force. David was always required to be on guard of the king's changeable mood. On more than one occasion David dodged his impulsively thrown javelin while playing music in the palace. Driven by repeated episodes of jealousy and rage, Saul relentlessly hounded him. David took refuge in the vast Judean wilderness. In desperation, he once feigned insanity, lodging in the streets of a Philistine city among the enemies of Israel. With Saul's army on his heels, he often found himself just a few steps away from being discovered, fleeing just on the other side of a desert hill or valley. He retreated to rock fortresses and to caves, hoping for a short period of safety and rest.

Through those difficult times God's eye and His protection was always upon David. On two occasions, Saul found himself unwittingly in David's hands, giving assurance of God's control and direction. The record of the kings of Israel provides the narration, but it is in the Psalms of David that the story of the heart is revealed. It was probably in caves that David wrote several of his Psalms, at least one or more in the cave of Adullam. For him it was a place of testing, forever watching for the enemy to return and find him out.

So it is with Lyme disease, forever wondering when the enemy will return and find you out — nowhere to flee and nowhere to hide. The constant tone in my left ear is a reminder of the ravages of Lyme disease, and it leaves one always looking for a period of rest as well. There is no way to turn off the sound which is continually generated inside my head. It goes on day and night, having gotten slowly louder since its inception during the first year of Lyme symptoms. It is present when falling asleep in the evening and it is there when waking in the middle of night. The only relief from it comes with the unexplainable ability of the brain to sometimes ignore the sound and allow the activities of daily thought to provide an escape from the consciousness of it for a while.

In the quietness of the cave, David spoke of God's comfort as he fought off fear and discouragement.

> When my spirit was overwhelmed within me ...
> ... There is no escape for me ...
> *(Psalms 142:3,4)*

The Bible tells of others who heard of his whereabouts and joined him there. Among them were those who were in distress, without resource, or bitter of soul (1 Samuel 22:2).

I was amazed to discover that all around me there were so many others touched by Lyme. One Lyme specialist told me that he treated about 100 patients each year from my area. Another in a different area told me that he had over

600 patients currently. Just as David came to realize the many others with a burdened soul, those with Lyme are also soon acquainted with the many stories of despair.

One of the Lyme specialists, with whom I consulted several times, often digressed in his conversation to a few of his favorite simple illustrations. On one occasion with the wave of his hands and a captivatingly serious grin, he colorfully narrated the scene of enemy invaders inside my body. "There is no way to completely eradicate or purge them," he explained with a certain realism. And there is nowhere for the cells of my body to hide. The enemy will find them.

The battle between the "good guys" and "bad guys", as he put it, seems endless as the immune system wages war and I am caught up in the conflict. But as the Psalmist wrote,

> I cried out to You, O LORD;
> I said, "You are my refuge …"
> *(Psalms 142:5)*

In Psalms 34:4, another Psalm possibly composed in a cave, David's heart is calmed,

> I sought the LORD, and He answered me,
> And delivered me from all my fears.

In the solitude of the cave David found God's comfort. It brought new strength to his soul, which would last throughout his life.

Adversity, if for no other reason, is of benefit, since it is sure to bring a season of sober reflection. People see clearer at such times. Storms purify the atmosphere.

— HENRY WARD BEECHER

Hope in the Midst of Despair

7

When you're in a Slump, you're not in for much fun.
Un-slumping yourself is not easily done.

— DR. SEUSS

By the middle of May it was time for another visit with Dr. B. I think he might have wanted to say, "I told you so." to all the things I had searched out and scratched off my list. But he was kind enough not to. Then I told him that I had heard of a neurologist not far away who was well known for investigating difficult cases of neurologic problems. But when he heard the name, his countenance changed in an instant. With a frown on his face and a resolute tone in his voice, he said, "If you go to that doctor, you *will* have MS disease." Well, I did not really want MS disease, so that afternoon I quietly canceled the appointment, which I had actually already made but not told him about.

However, before this visit was over, he confessed that he was about at the end of his skills to help me and graciously offered to refer me to Mayo Clinic. As if he had been thinking about it for a while, he had all the details laid out, including the location, procedure, cost, and what to expect. I had already given some thought to this myself as well, pondering the services offered and how it might help me. But considering the disillusionment that I was now experiencing with modern medicine, I was having a hard time embracing it as a greater hope.

Seeing that I was not quite ready for this, he inserted an alternative at this carefully chosen moment. There was a neurologist at the university medical center in another city nearby that he greatly respected. And for a fraction of the time and cost, he argued, an appointment with him could be arranged. It took little convincing. I agreed and he made the preparations for the following month.

In the meantime the month of May continued on. And I continued on, meticulously filling in with fine print the numbered squares on the calendar with daily symptoms until the words were overflowing into the margins. The last week, just before Memorial Day, was another scheduled business trip, this time to Virginia Beach. I decided to take my wife and youngest son along since they had wanted to see the nearby sites which we had not had an opportunity in the past to visit. Almost each night was the same, nerve shocks in the head, light headed. Lying in bed, surrounded by darkness, staring at the ceiling of the hotel suite, I sensed that there was quietness out there somewhere ... but not inside my head.

I had developed a sensation that I came to call "hyperacusis". But I always felt compelled to explain when I used the term that it is not what the word may first convey. Like many people, I would think that as the name suggests, it refers to a condition in which hearing is more acute or amplified. However, that confusing misnomer is not really possible. Hearing is not made more sensitive in that one hears sounds with any greater ability, but rather, that even a low level sound triggers the otherwise spontaneous nerve shocks in the head.

So, one is more sensitive to sounds only in that they cause painfully disturbing repetitive auditory nerve sensations. They are sometimes almost as irritating as the shrill feedback oscillation of a microphone, turned too loud. The single ding of a microwave timer far way in the kitchen was enough to trigger the sensation. So the ear is "hyper" sensitive, particularly to any sudden, staccato sound, setting off the hair trigger of the nerves connected to the auditory system. Just as I might gain a moment of relaxation this condition became an unwelcome reminder of the under surface turmoil.

Walking through the streets of reconstructed Williamsburg and Jamestown, I struggled among the many costumed characters and looked frequently for a place to rest my weak legs and body. I welcomed the small gatherings where performers staged a reenactment giving opportunity to find a spot to sit for a few minutes. It was as if I could, with enough determination, go and do the things that I would normally choose but with extraordinary effort. And I did not fully run out of energy but perpetually required complete exertion to keep going. I felt like an Energizer Bunny in which someone had unwittingly installed "ACME" batteries. Everything ran in slow motion. It was like a bad dream in which one cannot escape because they are always just short of collapse but never exhausted. Some inner drive in me just kept going, as if to resist the inevitable, but wondering why the inevitable was so long in coming. Surely I could not go on like this, and yet I did.

Yes, I made it through the month of May and turned to a fresh page on my calendar. I wondered if it would be filled to the brim with notes as the last page had been. One of the last appointments on the agenda given to me by Dr. B was with a respiratory specialist to check out my persistent throat irritation. This doctor was clearly focused, without the slightest hint of a stray rebellious thought, one that might lead to an analysis or conclusion which deviated from the norm. As with most of the doctors that I had seen, he found nothing unusual from his tests, but was prone to make some kind of diagnosis based on my clinical symptoms. His imagination came up with chronic bronchitis and he offered a prescription or two.

A few weeks later I got a call from my health insurance company sympathizing with me about my COPD condition and offering help from a support group. I was quite surprised to hear that I had COPD. That was a new one. I politely explained that I did not have COPD. Thinking a bit, I realized that the respiratory doctor must have added that to my diagnosis just for good measure.

One bright morning in the middle of June, I awoke much earlier than usual to get ready for a long drive. It was the day of my 8:00 am appointment with the neurologist that Dr. B had recommended. I tried not to get my hopes up, but it was indeed the last appointment that I had scheduled from Dr. B. Only blank pages were left on my calendar. The downtown streets were crowded but parking was available close by the medical office building, which was part of the university medical center. There was all around a sense of medical research going on, with spirited minds, that may have had greater insights in consideration of my case.

I did not have long to wait before being led to an exam room. It looked familiar to that of the neurologist that I had previously seen. He listened to my story as I mentioned my family doctor and his referral, hoping that he would take more interest in me, knowing that I had puzzled so many doctors before him. He appeared to meet the challenge as he proceeded with more nerve conduction tests of his own. He was for the most part close-lipped while working, except for some brief casual remarks. When he was completely finished, he asked a few more questions and then succinctly wrapped up his conclusion. "I wish all of my patients were in as good of shape as you are," he said. "Go and live your life". As I walked out to my car and drove out of the city, I pondered what my future held. It was as if this was the final statement from modern medicine — There was nothing wrong with me, at least not anything they could detect or do anything about.

Bible scholars differ in their opinions on the authorship of Psalms 116. Some attribute it to David, while others believe that it was written by Hezekiah, king of Judah, following his near fatal illness. Clearly it expresses the thoughts of someone who has been through a time of deep distress, uncertain of their survival. Verse 3 captures the anguish,

> The cords of death encompassed me
> And the terrors of Sheol came upon me;
> I found distress and sorrow.

The Hebrew word for "cords" is *chebel*. In context it conveys a sense of pain, sorrow, or destruction.

With Lyme disease, one often encounters dozens of doctors who have no clue as to the cause for the multitude of symptoms. Upon the eventual realization that modern medicine can offer no confidence or comfort, a cloud of hopeless darkness closes in like a dense fog in the night hours. Many of the individual symptoms could be life-threatening if they continued for a long enough time or if they worsen in intensity. There is a persistent recurring mental challenge to decide whether to give up or keep trying to find answers. But answers remain elusive.

In his affliction, confined by illness to his bed, Hezekiah "turned his face to the wall and prayed to the LORD". The Lord delivered Hezekiah and his heart was filled with praise.

> I love the LORD, because He hears
> My voice *and* my supplications.
> Because He has inclined His ear to me,
> Therefore I shall call *upon Him* as long
> as I live.
> *(Psalms 116:1,2)*

Despair is transformed into hope when we call upon the Lord. And it becomes a lasting hope for the future, growing richer with time, as we dwell on His faithfulness. Rather than the limitations of modern medicine, which bring a sense of discouragement, the limitless strength of the Lord brings continual hope and en-couragement.

> *When the wind blows hard on a tree, the roots stretch and grow the stronger.*
> — AMY CARMICHAEL

End of Self

8

Never worry about tomorrow, Charlie Brown. Tomorrow will soon be today, and before you know it, today will be yesterday! I always worry about the day after tomorrow!
— CHARLES SHULTZ

Some of my symptoms, particularly the chest spasms and heart palpitations had begun to lessen by the second half of June and it became a good excuse to take a break from the intense medical pursuit. My attention was on the fall horizon. Since May I had plans for a business trip to Israel in October. I was very much looking forward to it. But always in the back of my mind there was the fear that this unknown menace would preempt such a trip. Pressing on through the summer, the tinnitus began to greatly increase along with the chest spasms and heart palpitations by September. When I mentioned the tinnitus to my dentist, he recommended checking it out with an oral surgeon to see if it was TMJ related. I visited the doctor that he suggested who after a brief examination of my jaw saw little to suspect such a cause. But he ordered an MRI just the same. Not surprisingly, it revealed nothing new.

When October arrived, I boarded the plane to Israel, confident that if I had gotten this far, I would make it through the trip. The 12 hour flight offered some short sleep as I tried to make myself comfortable among the long rows of seats. I took my mind off the lingering spasms and nerve excitation by staring at the flight display on the back of the seat in front of me. I watched with unreserved anticipation as the small icon in the shape of a plane almost imperceptibly moved, propelled by a line which trailed from its tail back to the point of origin in Atlanta. And I watched as the marker for Tel Aviv drew closer and closer. With determination I pushed my symptoms out of my consciousness for the next 6 days until I approached the airport to return.

For once the importance of the present was greater than the sum of all my physical symptoms. I walked and talked, carried on my business, and viewed the sights before me. As I walked through the streets of Jerusalem once again and strolled along the cobblestones of Joppa near the hotel, I enjoyed the time with a thankful heart.

The same symptoms continued off and on throughout the end of the year. By the end of the following winter, however, there was a noticeable decline in the primary nerve symptoms except for the tinnitus, which remained in my left ear. I dared not consider that the mysterious illness was permanently resolving. For when I did it would invariably remind me of its presence with the spontaneous recurrence of various symptoms as if they were jealous of my tranquility. Nevertheless, there was some notable relief for a period of time. This lasted until late summer of 2011. Then I began to have an ache in the chest, which I first surmised was just a respiratory infection.

After several weeks without relief, I visited Dr. B again. Although I had not seen him for over a year, I was a bit surprised that he appeared to have put all of my previous troubles totally of out of his head, along with the many maddening mysteries of medicine. Or at least if they still lurked somewhere in the back of his mind, he certainly had done an enviable job of muzzling them. He did not mention the past year at all, but just listened politely as always. At the end of my short description and his examination, He seemed puzzled, finding nothing out of the ordinary with my lungs or chest. He waxed on for a few minutes as if thinking out loud about the possibilities. I could see the gears turning, but nothing enlightening came forth. Finally, he ordered an x-ray and gave me a prescription for antibiotics just in case.

It took about 3 more weeks before the chest ache was much improved on its own. And it was only then upon reflection I realized that the residual chest spasms, which had been masked somewhat by the ache were too much like the symptoms that plagued me months before to be coincidental. It was beginning to return. And so it did as the fall season began.

Staying busy generally helped, and throughout life, "busy" never seemed to have any trouble finding me. Only now however, my usual tireless pace was beginning to be *tired* and *less*. Among the many projects accumulating on my perpetual list was the remodeling of an attic space over the garage. The attic had collected 26 years of trash and treasures. There was no room to keep it all. Over the next few weeks I spent night after night in the dim light unearthing each stack or pile. There were boxes teetering higher than my shoulders, and old chests of drawers so full they were hard to wrestle open without risking the well being of my fingers in the process. I carried a fly swatter in one hand, never knowing what I was about to encounter, face to face. Fortunately, it was only wasps and spiders. I am not sure what I would have done with such a weapon if I had discovered anything moving that was larger.

The history of my life was scattered before me in every hidden space, slowly pulled from the darkness of its container. With each object uncovered came the need for a decision of what to keep and what to let go. The past year and a half had taken its toll. I began to place more and more items in the pile to let go. Boxes of papers from college, antique electronics that I had plans to one day restore, my photographic equipment — all of it had a story to tell and it was speaking much too loudly at the moment.

I pondered the uncertainty of my long term future, and the possibility of never solving the mystery of my condition was like an ever growing weight. Stooping there in the narrow makeshift aisles among the crowded boxes and dusty furniture, I relinquished my hold on those material objects as if they were my last grip on life. I was ready to let go if for no other reason than to ease the mental ache. The memories attached to them were now so intense that I had to fight off the sadness. And as I did I reached desperately for a well worn thought called ... *thankfulness.*

I carried the many bulging boxes and other items down the stairs to load into the back of my truck. Within the next week I selected a couple of people who might be interested in these things, including one friend of many years. I emptied box after box of papers into the trash and with each one, I relinquished a little more of myself. It was hard to let some of these things go, but at the same time it was a relief to let the hold on my life go with them and turn the future over to God. Finally the attic was empty and a part of me was as well.

During the socially tumultuous years of college I frequently sat down on my dorm room bed and set my bible next to me. As I opened it the pages would, as if from memory, fold over on one side or the other. This invisible place holder led me straight to my go-to verse. Dark stains at the margin's edge gave evidence of the countless times that my thumbs rested there. On the left hand leaf, a little more than half way down in the second column, the words were underlined in red ink.

> "... for truly I say to you, if you have faith the size of a mustard seed, you will say to this mountain, 'Move from here to there,' and it will move; and nothing will be impossible to you."
> *(Matthew 17:20b)*

I could have recited the verse, but there was something about seeing the words and reading each one over several times that gave me assurance that the promise was still good. I could sense that the Lord was sitting beside me in that quiet room. It never grew old to rest in that silent peace.

Little did I know then that nearly 30 years later I would find myself actually standing at a place where Jesus had stood while voicing this illustration. With the hot sun bearing down on my face, the scene offered fresh insight into this repeated reference of the mountain to be moved. To understand it more fully another verse, a few chapters later, in Matthew 21:21 helps with the context. During the final week of Jesus' ministry He and His disciples trekked along the same path each day. It led them along the edge of the Mount of Olives between Bethany, where they stayed, and the temple in Jerusalem. On the third morning as they walked this same way into the city, the disciples noticed the withered fig tree that Jesus had spoken against the day before because it did not bear fruit. Jesus took the opportunity to teach His disciples another lesson about faith.

> And Jesus answered and said to them, "Truly I say to you, if you have faith and do not doubt, you will not only do what was done to the fig tree, but even if you say to this mountain, 'Be taken up and cast into the sea,' it will happen."

The edge of the road drops off sharply, and from the precipice may be seen the low hills of the Judean desert to the south. Conspicuously rising above these hills about 7.5

miles in the distance is a mountain with the remains of a uniquely circular depression on the top. This man-made mountain was constructed by Herod the Great. During the early first century, while in its full splendor, a magnificent round palace towered high above the top of the mountain. It was designed to be the highest structure seen as one gazed over the hills from the Mount of Olives, and even today the ruins convey what was once a formidable sight. It was an inescapable reminder to each passerby of all that was despised by the Jews. It represented a world that *overpowered the body, solicited fear in the mind, and promoted a sense of defeat in the soul.*

A mustard seed is so small that it can be lost in a crease of skin as you hold it in the palm of your hand. Yet even just this much God-given faith could overcome all that tormented them. It would be buried in the sea. What sea? Well, far off, near the horizon to the southeast, visible on a clear day from this vantage point at the top of the Mount of Olives, is the small shimmering reflection of the Dead Sea. As the disciples turned their heads they could easily grasp the full illustration as Jesus spoke. The menace would be dropped to the depths of the abyss. Just a tiny faith can do this according to Jesus' words.

I found that Lyme disease had much in common with the fortress of Herod. *Its symptoms overpower the body, its uncertainty solicits fear in the mind, and its sense of abandonment promotes defeat in the soul.* I longed to cast it into the abyss.

Is it better to have a tiny faith in a big God or a lot of faith in a small god? Often we chose the latter when we should be exercising the former. To exercise the faith that God gives us we must use it to empower our *trust* in God. Anything that requires exercise requires time. And it requires a continual renewal of that which motivates it.

On still another occasion, while travelling with the disciples leaving Galilee on the way to Jerusalem, Jesus used the illustration of the mustard seed to demonstrate the power of faith. As recorded in the Gospel of Luke, the disciples had perhaps been listening for hours to many of the hard lessons of life and living as Jesus taught along the way. Finally, their silence was broken with their exclamation,

> The apostles said to the Lord, "Increase our faith!"
> *(Luke 17:5)*

Without hesitation Jesus replies in the next verse,

> And the Lord said, "If you had faith like a mustard seed, you would say to this mulberry tree, 'Be uprooted and be planted in the sea'; and it would obey you."

The disciples knew that faith comes from God. If they desired more, they needed to ask for it. But Jesus wanted them to understand that faith is very powerful, even a little, if it is exercised in *trust*. ***Faith grows as we are granted more of it from God, but its power increases the more we grant to God our trust.***

So then, as the 19th century American clergyman, William Plumer once asked, *"Why are we so slow to trust an infinite God?"* Jesus understood the frailty of the human heart, which longs to respond to the persuasion of God, but continually struggles against fearful doubts. It is truly a tug-of-war between the mind and the soul. The story is told in the Gospel of Mark of a man with a son possessed by an unclean spirit that had tormented the boy since he was a young child. Having an opportune moment of Jesus' attention, the father pleaded for His help, as the disciples had been unable to cure the boy.

> "But if You can do anything, take pity on us and help us!"
> *(Mark 9:22b)*

Jesus' response revealed the father's inner turmoil, which so often besets our attempts to trust God.

> And Jesus said to him, "'If You can?' All things are possible to him who believes." Immediately the boy's father cried out and said, "I do believe; help my unbelief."
> *(Mark 9:23,24)*

Our faith tells us that God can do anything, but our heart cries out for help to trust Him. The outspokenness of the Apostle Peter made him very transparent. During Jesus' ministry Peter's belief sometimes got ahead of his actions and his faith often got ahead of his trust.

Shortly after a great miracle where Jesus fed 5000 people, the disciples found themselves in a boat, rowing wearily against strong winds and waves in the Sea of Galilee for most of the night. In their effort to travel to a nearby shore, they had only managed to go a few miles when Jesus suddenly appeared, walking on the water toward their boat. First, overcome by fright, the disciples then recognized who it was. Peter boldly requested to walk out of the boat to Jesus. But soon after taking a few steps, his trust melted with the consciousness of the roaring wind around him.

> ... he cried out, "Lord, save me!" Immediately Jesus stretched out His hand and took hold of him, and said to him, "You of little faith, why did you doubt?"
> *(Matthew 14:30,31)*

The Greek word translated "little faith" is *oligopistos*. It is a combination of two Greek words; used together they simply mean "trusting too little". The word translated doubt, *distazo*, also is a combination of two Greek words. The first is *dis*, which means "two, double". The second is *stasis*, which means "stance". So together it is "double-stance", one who vacillates or wavers, one who halts between two choices. In the midst of the roaring wind and surging waves there are two choices. We will either place our trust in God or trust in human nature. The tug of human nature is always strong, but trust in God is always sure.

Chronic mystery illnesses such as Lyme disease can bring with them wave after wave of wavering doubt. It is easy to vacillate and halt with every lingering uncertainty. There seems to never be closure, but only more reason to doubt. As our doubt is exposed, we, like Peter may also cry out to the Lord. And He will stretch out His hand to hold us up. Once they were in the boat, the sea was calm. The disciples had previously rowed through the night in the storm tossed boat, watching the shore line and making little progress. But the lesson they eventually learned before the night was over would not soon be forgotten. It would remind them countless times later when they faced a doubting situation in life. And so it is with Lyme disease. One is reminded countless times later on to take the Lord's hand without hesitation.

> *It is safer on the waves with Jesus than in the boat without Him.*
>
> — ADRIAN ROGERS

Providence Revealed

"And how are you?" said Winnie-the-Pooh. Eeyore shook his head from side to side. "Not very how," he said. "I don't seem to have felt at all how for a long time."
— A.A. MILNE

entle breezes and cooler evenings had begun to arrive, suggesting that the seasons were about to change. I happened to pick up a Christian magazine from the forever growing stack near the head of my bed to catch up on some reading. It was published by the Home School Legal Defense Association (HSLDA). As I flipped through the articles, my eyes caught something which grabbed my attention. It was a segment by Dr. Roger Sayre, a family practice physician in Tunkhannock, Pennsylvania, who wrote for the magazine. It told of his newly found understanding of the puzzling symptoms exhibited by some of his patients.

For years he had misdiagnosed what he now realized was Lyme disease. As I read further he mentioned some of the symptoms, and the more I read the more I was riveted to the article. The resemblance of these symptoms to mine was remarkable. My mind was racing as he revealed the failure of popular tests for the disease. Pausing for a moment, I soon realized that I had been living under an illusion for the past 18 months.

As the article continued, the doctor apologized for his misguidance to his former patients. He advised that people with these symptoms seek out a "Lyme literate" doctor in order to be evaluated. The article provided the name of an organization which could help with recommendations. I wasted no time locating the names of doctors. There were very few in my entire region, but I located one about 350 miles away.

It was none too soon. My symptoms had returned with intensity over the next few days. The following week I was out of town again on a business trip to Baltimore. I had become very weak and the nerve shocks were now very prevalent night and day. I tried several times to reach the recommended doctor but got only an answering machine. Finally, in desperation I took out my cell phone and tried once again while passing through a parking lot on the way to my car as I left one meeting and headed for another that afternoon. With a colleague patiently waiting for me in the car, the doctor's nurse picked up the phone on the other end. For a brief second I imagined that my call must have been routed to an angelic switchboard in heaven. I learned later that the nurse rarely answered the phone during the day in this small office, and her busy day as the only nurse often resulted in the phone messages being backed up for many days.

I could only breathe a prayer of thankfulness as I related my story and told her that I would like to get an appointment. Her first question was, "Are you able to walk?" "What a strange question," I thought. Then I realized that apparently some of the patients that they see with the disease must be in considerably worse condition. I was glad to reply that I could walk and would take any appointment time available. Suddenly I had a new hope! I floated through the rest of the day.

Just over two weeks to wait. It was not easy. I spent the time going back over all of my notes. With engineering precision, I reformatted and reorganized the information, chronicling the myriad of symptoms, listing all the tests, and the long list of doctors and specialties. Finally the day came. It was the first week of October. With my wife along we left at dawn to allow plenty of time for the 1:00 pm appointment. Making only a few brief stops along the way we arrived near the office with some time to spare. So, we paused for lunch just across the street. I was both anxious and eager at the same time. We navigated the medical complex and found the building. Up the elevator and down the hall we journeyed until we located the small office front. Entering the non-descript waiting room I met the nurse behind the glass window with whom I had previously talked. After the usual papers to fill out, I took a seat. That is when I noticed, with a smile, the silk screened T-shirt hanging by the counter. It read, "If life gives you Lyme, make limeade".

One patient was seated across the room ahead of me to see the doctor. There was only a minute or two before he was called in, just time for a few casual remarks, but enough to recognize from his comments that he too had struggled with many strange symptoms. One of which he whimsically illustrated as the sound of squirrels running around in his head. I must confess that I was glad to not to have that symptom as strange images flashed through my imagination for a brief second.

The time on the clock now seemed to greatly slow down. At first I thought it was just me. However, after considerably more time had passed I had to remind myself that there was only one other patient in the office. I wondered why it was taking so long. At that moment the nurse emerged. As if somehow aware of my observation, she explained that the doctor spends a lot of time with his patients, and that I should be assured, it will be worth the wait since he will spend ample time with me as well. I smiled again and nodded to her.

Finally, the door opened and the other patient emerged, apparently quite pleased with the outcome of his visit. He encouraged me that I would be pleased also, although he alerted me that the doctor was quite unusual in some ways. He wished me well, and shortly the nurse welcomed me back to the exam room after the requisite weigh in. The doctor was a spry man both physically and in his speech as well. His decades of experience, both in medicine and in life overflowed as he spoke. With a slight squint of the eye he shifted from one subject to the next in casual but sometimes hurried conversation. He had an outspoken opinion on a wide range of topics and seemed intent on conveying each, from raising children to government taxes. He continued to do so at every opportunity, all the while proceeding with his examination and occasionally typing on a computer keyboard.

After commenting on the meticulous nature of my notes, which I had passed along to him in advance through the nurse, he allowed me to speak. So without delay I began to review what was now over an 18 month medical history of symptoms and doctors and testing. I zeroed in on the symptoms, using my relatively simple word descriptions. But before I could verbalize more than the first few, he interrupted almost in sync with my recitation. One by one he named the rest, as if he read my mind. Furthermore, he added his own word description with some of them. My favorite was what I had called head shocks for lack of a more elegant term; he coined, "zingers". I immediately grasped and adopted that term. It was so perfectly descriptive. How could he know? I could do nothing but sit there, listening with what must have been a very surprised look on my face. I think I did manage a simple "Yes" as he finished the description.

From then on he took over much of the conversation, providing me with a wealth of new information. After a lengthy speech with an occasional joke to break the rhythm, he concluded that based on my clinical symptoms, he was convinced I had Lyme disease or a related co-infection. I was never so glad to hear that I had a disease! He sent me off for some blood tests of his own including a Western Blot Lyme test which is generally much more reliable than other tests. However, he cautioned that because I had been on antibiotics and much time had passed, it was very likely that the test result would be negative.

Nonetheless, he planned his treatment for Lyme, which included some modest antibiotics over the course of the coming year. He predicted that if successful, I should start to see improvements within a few months and resolution of almost all symptoms within 1-2 years. He was much less promising about the tinnitus however, indicating that it may not resolve due to permanent auditory nerve damage.

Then he added, really the only way to verify that the Lyme infection was totally eradicated would be to cut the body up into small pieces and evaluate the DNA of each cell individually since residual bacteria could hide anywhere. The broad, narrow grin on his face, shaded by his gray eyebrows suggested that he may have thought about that idea a little more than one ought.

Over the next 3-4 months the symptoms did slowly decrease. A few more visits to the doctor's office throughout the following year with a couple of adjustments to the medication resulted in almost insignificant symptoms, with just some mild residual episodes. However, the tinnitus remained, seemingly untouched by the treatment. By now I had learned to live with the constant tone in the left ear, ignoring it as much as possible. There were a few occasions when it would disappear for a short period of an hour of so, and it was a special blessing to experience complete silence again, even if it were brief. I would just stop what I was doing and thank the Lord any time I experienced one of those quiet moments. It prompted me to be thankful for all blessings, especially the resolution of so many other symptoms.

With my final visit to the Lyme specialist I was ready to enjoy life again. I still kept my calendar journal. But by the time my treatment ended in the fall of 2012, there were only a few entries each month. I assumed these short episodes of chest spasms and "zingers" were also residual nerve damage.

Almost two years later, in the fall of 2014, however, the symptoms returned with intensity and duration that were more pronounced. Lasting for a couple of months, I decided to contact the Lyme specialist for a visit. He ran more blood tests and I returned home to wait for the results. He contacted me by email to say that the tests were normal and offered no other help. Suddenly I felt alone again. I had reached the end of the life line that I had so cherished. What would I do now? I reread the email over and over hoping for some other conclusion to somehow appear from the stark words on my computer screen. But it didn't. If the symptoms did not subside again with time, I had no course of action to seek. I had already exhausted every other possible solution. And now it appeared that if the Lyme disease had been resolved, than something else may still be the problem.

Not knowing what more to do, I waited, or more honestly, endured for another month or two. The symptoms slowly receded. Overtaken by life's activities, I accepted feeling better and continued staying busy for almost a year. Near the end of 2015 the symptoms returned again. Only this time they were more intense and longer lasting than before. My wife and I had been planning a trip to Florida. I was hoping that the change would bring some relief. Upon arriving, however, the chest spasms, tremors and heart palpitations were so severe at night that I thought about abbreviating our trip and returning home. But the next night was slightly better, and we were able to remain. I scheduled an appointment to see my family doctor soon after returning.

Dr. B had retired and so this would be a first time experience for both me and the new doctor. When I met her I realized that she had only a few years of clinical practice. I wondered if her medical training was from the same textbook as so many other doctors that I had met. I summarized the history of my condition, and then cautiously mentioned Lyme disease. I paused for an almost imperceptible period to observe the reaction in her facial expression. I was pleasantly surprised when I saw no sign of disdain. Perhaps she had not taken that course in medical school. I tried not to let my apprehension show as I continued. She conceded her lack of familiarity with Lyme disease, but recommended some routine tests. She also set up an appointment with a rheumatologist, one of the few remaining specialists that I had not yet seen to check out any possible autoimmune disorders.

The visit to the rheumatologist was innocuous enough, but he only repeated tests that had previously been taken, and when I mentioned Lyme disease symptoms, it was clear that the light was not on. I later viewed his report, written to my family doctor. And when I read that he had most politely referred to me as a "pleasant gentleman" for whom he could find no cause of the symptoms, I well knew that it was time to go back to her for a follow-up visit.

With a little more research I had learned that other Lyme specialists do not consider the late stage disease to likely be eliminated completely by antibiotic treatment. This would explain the recurrences. So I located another Lyme specialist who maintained this opinion and decided to rejoin my quest. However, this doctor was quite busy and my first attempt at an appointment proved unsuccessful. I appealed to my family doctor to aid in getting a referral. Without much persuasion she was receptive to the request, soon gaining an appointment for me. But it was still a long wait, nearly 7 months away before I would see the specialist.

I decided to spend the time researching the treatment approach that this doctor was known to practice. It involved, in part, some non-prescription supplements. For the next months before the appointment I experimented with some of these in the hope of at least learning their possible benefits, and perhaps even gaining some relief from the symptoms. All in all there was minimal benefit from these supplements over the summer and early fall. When October arrived, with my appointment close at hand, the anticipation began to mount. Again I prepared my copious notes, placing them into a thick file folder and made extra copies for the doctor.

Adversities are often unexpected, hence the line, "when adversity strikes". Medically related adversities are no exception. More often than not, it seems they come with some element of surprise. James 1:2 tells us to, "Consider it all Joy" when adversities come. 1 Thessalonians 5:18 says, "In everything give thanks". But sometimes it is hard to be thankful for that kind of joy. James continues on in verses 2-4 to explain,

> ... when you encounter various trials, knowing that the testing of your faith produces endurance. And let endurance have its perfect result, so that you may be perfect and complete, lacking in nothing.

Not if, but *when* these trials, as they are called, venture upon us, we are told that they bring with them the opportunity to exercise our faith. In so doing there is something in particular that is produced or generated in the process. It is called here "endurance". This is the same Greek word mentioned earlier in 2 Peter 1, which is sometimes translated "steadfastness". But to be steadfast we need something in which to stand fast. The next verse drives this thought home. Steadfastness leads to a result. And the result is that we become perfect and complete, lacking in nothing. To lack for nothing implies that we are supplied with everything that we need. And therefore we depend on something or someone to provide all of our needs. That someone is God.

Webster defines the word "trust" simply as,

> Assured reliance on the character, ability, strength, or truth of someone or something.

This steadfastness, which results from the exercise of our faith causes us to depend more completely on God, or we might say to *trust* in God. The Greek word for faith used here is *pistis*. It means to persuade or be persuaded or to "persuade to *trust*". The concept of faith is not so simple as is the definition of trust. Faith is a much broader concept. The Greek translation of the Old Testament, called the Septuagint, uses this same Greek word for seven different Hebrew words of various related meanings. It is the predominate word used for "faith" in the New Testament.

This act of persuasion, which is inherent in faith is always given or produced by God, not man. We have the capacity to exercise this gift and when we do, we are told that it will produce trust in God. Understanding the difference between these two, faith, or the persuasion to trust, and trust itself is key to gaining what James calls completeness or maturity as a Christian through adversity. Faith is God's work in and through us. Our ongoing trust in God is the result.

Trusting God is not easy. But it begins with reminding ourselves of what it means and then recognizing it as an essential goal, allowing it to impact our thinking. We are first prone to trust ourselves, as is our nature. But Proverbs 3:5,6 instructs,

> Trust in the LORD with all your heart
> And do not lean on your own understanding.
> In all your ways acknowledge Him,
> And He will make your paths straight.

We are told to trust in the Lord with all our heart, without reservation, without concern, without worry, without depending upon ourselves. But this kind of compete trust comes at the persuasion of the God given faith that is in us. It is not natural. It is hard to perfect. The adversities of life are tough tools for a tough job. They are used by God to aid in this process.

It is faith alone that persuades us to salvation and it is faith alone that persuades us to trust in God. How sweet that trust is when once attained. This verse from Solomon is not a pious platitude. It is an insightful instruction. It advises to not lean on our own thoughts and doing. But it is not an admonition to have no thoughts or take no actions. We are not to give up. There is a fine line between trusting God and testing God (Deuteronomy 6:16). Through the application of trust we find God's direction as we acknowledge or recognize His thoughts and deeds.

Undoubtedly Solomon grew up with many memories of the psalms written and spoken by his father, King David. Trusting in God was a regular theme. So, Solomon's words carry with them not only his wisdom from God, but also convey the experience of David's trust through many dark and difficult times. The paths made straight were real and well worn. The refrain of Psalms 37:4,5 comes from the heart of King David's life among his daily battles, spoken with very similar words,

Delight yourself in the LORD;
And He will give you the desires of your heart.

Commit your way to the LORD,
Trust also in Him ...

Often my first reflection upon consciously arriving at that blissful state is to take notice of the sense of "peace", not unlike the calm of nature after a storm. The prophet Isaiah voiced this well in the words of his song of praise to the Lord,

The steadfast of mind You will
keep in perfect peace,
Because he trusts in You.
(Isaiah 26:3)

I regularly wondered whether to continue the pursuit of my health difficulties with the search for diagnosis and further treatment options, or to abandon the effort and just leave it to God to either heal or not. Almost as if living out the words of an older Solomon, I found myself alternately giving myself to the effort or withdrawing from it.

There is an appointed time for everything ...
A time to throw stones and a time to gather stones;
A time to embrace and a time to shun embracing.
A time to search and a time to give up as lost;
A time to keep and a time to throw away.
(Ecclesiastes 3:1,5,6)

I found myself at times embracing and gathering and searching and keeping in my efforts. At other times my path ran quietly still and left me waiting, leaning on God. I soon found that trust over the course of time demanded both.

> *God walks with us. He scoops us up in His arms or simply sits with us in silent strength until we cannot avoid the awesome recognition that yes, even now, He is there.*
>
> — GLORIA GAITHER

Peace, Be Still

Give me a moment, because I like to cry for joy. It's so delicious… to cry for joy.

— CHARLES DICKENS

I t was a 200 mile drive that fall afternoon to visit the Lyme specialist. My wife and I planned to leave a day early with plenty of time the next morning to arrive for the 10:30 am appointment on Wednesday. The doctor reserved Wednesdays for his Lyme patients which allowed for adequate time with each one. But with such an accommodation comes the rather long wait in the office. As we walked in, I was handed some paperwork to fill out, and noticed a man in a white coat who stood far behind the counter. He was at first engaged with other matters, so I was not expecting it when he raised his hand to wave in my direction. Looking around, I was not sure his gesture was intended for me, but soon realized that in the sparse room behind me, there could be no one else in his view. I realized that it was the doctor that I had come to see. By now he had disappeared into the maze of doors far in the background.

Eventually a nurse appeared and I tagged along behind, only to wait again for an extended period in the exam room. The door must have been very thick because I could hear very little outside. When the doctor walked in with his curly hair and jolly smile, my attention was soon focused on him. He let me talk for a short while, and then for the next hour or so he did most of the talking. When I really had something that I wanted to say or ask, it was necessary to pace his words for an opportune moment before quickly interrupting. It was like trying to get on a moving merry-go-round with an eye on one particular horse, eager for just the right second to leap up and on. Otherwise, I sensed that I would break his entire train of thought.

Such interruptions did allow me to occasionally adjust the trail of the conversation to topics of most interest to me, among the overwhelming amount of information being spoken. He drifted from one medical point to another and threw in an anecdote or two now and then. I took a few notes while he wrote down a few notes for me as well, which he handed to me before leaving.

The doctor reinforced the notion that I had recently come to understand. Once you have late stage Lyme or other co-infection, you are not likely to ever completely eradicate it. So treatment involves various options from antibiotics to supplements to dietary or other life style changes. He gave me some specific alternatives, including a recommendation for a round of antibiotic treatment to start, promising to send a prescription. But first, he wanted to try again with another more detailed Western Blot DNA test to see if he could verify the Lyme infection. My questions were not all fully answered, but I saw him look at his watch with heightened anxiety. He quickly voiced his goodbye's and hastily exited the room with the same jolly smile, as his coat tail trailed behind him through the door.

Although more antibiotics were not what I had hoped for, at least I had a plan and a doctor with Lyme experience who understood my repeatedly recurring symptoms. So, I rested in that thought as we drove the long road home. Even though there was much uncertainty ahead, it was a comforting feeling, in which I lost no time to savor.

Over the next weeks the report from the most recent Lyme test came back with a positive result. But my symptoms had very gradually become relatively mild again. I reasoned that maybe I would wait until they were more pronounced before venturing into the stronger antibiotics recommended by the doctor. So, with that clever and sharp-witted logic, much of 2017 passed by. At the end of the summer my symptoms emerged again, this time with even greater vengeance. Finally, I decided to start the antibiotics, which required a considerable amount of daily management, owing to so many bottles and timing requirements for each one. I felt like a most untalented circus juggler trying desperately to keep a dozen objects in the air without them landing on my nose. Week by week and month by month, the raging symptoms continued.

We kept our date with another planned trip to Florida while I limped along. I wondered how long one's heart would take such an onslaught, sometimes skipping every other beat for hours at a time. My chest ached from the ordeal. The "zingers" joined the chorus. The antibiotics ended just after Thanksgiving Day as the bottom of each bottle at last appeared. The symptoms, however, showed no sign of relenting. The new year came as the symptoms had raged for 4 months, and still increasing in strength. It would be almost another 2-3 months before they finally began to subside. In the meantime I had tried desperately to get an appointment with my family doctor. Finally, a few days before Christmas, I was able see her and she referred me to a cardiologist for a repeat of the regiment of tests to verify that my heart was still ok.

Now with a history of Lyme diagnosis, this most recent cardiologist was at least receptive to my condition, although not particularly knowledgeable of the disease. He again verified that my heart was fine, and could only offer a prescription to possibly help with the symptoms. But as usual, his choice of medication was useless for my condition, and into the zip lock bag it soon went. The bag by the way, was now bulging in every direction and required considerable effort to zip.

The Lyme specialist used email to help communicate with his patients. I tried to keep each message brief, knowing that he had hundreds of other Lyme patients in addition to his remaining practice. Often it took several days to hear from him and his messages were hardly more than a line or two written with cryptic abbreviations as if a text message.

It sometimes took me a while to decipher them as there were errors from his hurry as well. I had kept him informed of my progress since I had started the antibiotics and near the end voiced my concern about the ongoing symptoms. With each message the time for a response grew longer. I realized that I needed to make another appointment with him if ever to gain further help.

After the first of the year, I contacted his office, but discovered that he was booked for many months. Persistently, I continued to inquire sympathetically with his receptionist until I was able to secure a slot early in the following month, only a few weeks hence. An extra measure of peace was added to my frayed demeanor that day as I began to plan for the trip.

The doctor had added Friday's as a second day of the week for appointments to his Lyme patient practice. My appointment was late in the afternoon, his last patient of the day. I knew the routine and made myself as comfortable as possible in the sterile looking chairs of the waiting room. I was not sure if an appointment at the end of the day was good or bad. I expected for this to be a shorter visit with just some recommendations for further treatment and med prescriptions for another round of antibiotics.

It had been over a year since I was last in his office, but we seemed to pick up just where we left off before. A few minutes later he was wound up and speaking fast again. With a greater abundance of anecdotes tossed in, he was again writing notes for me while speaking. He encouraged me to consider some recommended supplements, which I had not heard him mention previously so I was not familiar

with them. He then handed me his notes, promised to send
the prescriptions, and looked at his watch. As if in a time
warp, he mimicked his exit from the last visit — worried
face, hurried goodbye's, jolly smile, and lightning retreat
through the door. Only this time I was able to slip in a few
extra words as we crossed paths one last time in the hallway
on our way out, wishing him well while he sped away for a
trip out of town that weekend.

As we usually did, my wife and I debriefed each other on
what we had learned and how to proceed while negotiating
the road home. I was now at a crossroads with two different possibilities — more meds or some new supplements. I
relayed the information to my sister, a nurse practitioner,
for her comments. And then I began to check out the supplements and eventually decided to order a Lyme specific
combination to try out. Along with this, my name ended
up on the supplier's list, and I started to receive additional
information on Lyme disease.

Among the various topics was a recommended diet plan,
which was strongly encouraged. It looked very austere, at
least for the early stages, designed for those with significant
digestive issues, which may contribute to the advancement
of Lyme symptoms. Although I did not have such issues,
I was ready to give it a try. My symptoms had begun to
stabilize by this time and were slowly diminishing. So, I
decided to continue with the supplements and diet changes
and reserve the antibiotics as a future option if needed.

Nearly a year passed and my condition further improved.
I eventually phased out most of the supplements for a while,
and my condition was still good. The diet changes remained

part of my daily routine as 2018 came to a close. And now my symptoms remain very mild. My future may never be free of Lyme disease, but in God's hands it will be freer than ever before.

The greatest awareness of peace is often when it is found in the midst of turmoil. While a stormy wind raged it violently tossed the small wooden craft in which the disciples huddled with fear and anxiety. Jesus was asleep in the back of the boat. He was at peace, knowing that all was under control. The waves washed dangerously over the sides, spilling water higher and higher inside. As the boat sank lower and the waves grew greater, the disciples awakened Jesus and said,

> "... Teacher [Master], do You not care that we are perishing?"
> *(Mark 4:38)*

Jesus arose and immediately spoke to the wind.

> ... and said unto the sea, "Peace, be still."
> *(Mark 4:39a) KJV*

The Greek word translated "peace" is a verb which means to be silent. There is a sublime, arresting silence in peace, which defies apt description.

> And the wind died down and it became per-
> fectly calm.
> *(Mark 4:39b)*

More literally, "there was a great calm". The sea was like glass, reflecting the dim light of the night against the sky. The silence was broken only by the sound of the water as it sloshed between the feet of the disciples. As their fear subsided they began to bail out the boat. The lingering calmness punctuated the sense of peace on the heels of the storm.

Jesus used the lesson to teach the disciples that He is the source of peace in the midst of the storm and that they have no reason to fear as long as He is with them. But Jesus also used the storm to show them by contrast what peace is really like. Certainly, there is nothing like the calm at the end of the storm to understand peace. But the real lesson that Jesus wanted them to learn is that there is peace to be found in the midst of the storm as well.

> When peace like a river attendeth my way,
>   When sorrows like sea billows roll;
> Whatever my lot Thou hast taught me to say,
>   "It is well, it is well with my soul!"
>   — HORATIO SPAFFORD,
>   *IT IS WELL WITH MY SOUL*

Lyme disease is often like the storm. The winds rage and the boat begins to fill up. It sometimes seems as though Jesus is sleeping in the back of the boat. We may be tempted to say to Him as the disciples did, "Do you care that I am perishing". But He just wants us to experience the indescribable peace that is found in the midst of the storm.

The apostle Paul wrote,

> And the peace of God, which surpasses all comprehension, will guard your hearts and your minds in Christ Jesus.
> *(Philippians 4:7)*

In verse 4 he prefaced this statement with the admonition,

> Rejoice in the Lord always; again I will say, rejoice!

The Greek verb for "rejoice" is *chairo*. It is cognate, which means that it shares the same root with two different Greek nouns. One is "joy" and the other is "grace". Therefore, they have the same core meaning. So the word for "rejoice" implies delighting in or experiencing or being conscious of God's grace. This is true joy! And with it comes a peace which is beyond words.

We can find this peace when, with thanksgiving in our heart, we seek God's help.

> Be anxious for nothing, but in everything by prayer and supplication with thanksgiving let your requests be made known to God.
> *(Philippians 4:6)*

The Greek word for "anxious", *merimnaó*, means to be torn apart. Lyme disease can tear one apart, not just physically, but mentally. God's peace will guard our hearts from thoughts that tug desperately in all directions, stretched between fear and hope.

The good, if it may be called that, of a disease like Lyme is in the prompting of verse 8,

> Finally, brethren, whatever is true, whatever is honorable, whatever is right, whatever is pure, whatever is lovely, whatever is of good repute, if there is any excellence and if anything worthy of praise, dwell on these things.

Herein is the secret to finding and keeping this unspeakable peace, "dwell on these things". If our joy is in such things as circumstances, amusements, friends, or health, it may soon be lost. Our joy is in the Lord when our thoughts are on Him.

In this world, full often, our joys are only the tender shadows which our sorrows cast.
— Henry Ward Beecher

Conclusion

That my soul may sing praise to You and not be silent.
O LORD my God, I will give thanks to You forever.
(Psalms 30:12)

The words of Psalms 30 voice King David's worshipful celebration of God's healing hand. Whether of a physical condition or spiritual healing at the mercy of God, we cannot be sure. But the occasion of this Psalm was the dedication of the "house", perhaps looking forward to the future house of the Lord for which David sought to prepare. With all the difficulties of life, David found reason for worship and praise. A song came to his heart and naturally flowed from his lips. It was a celebration of thanksgiving mingled with life's pain. For it is in those times that God gives a song.

Most often a song of praise is heard by others and shared so. With such praise God's mercies and grace are shared along with life's lessons learned. And I have learned a few. As C. S. Lewis once said,

> God allows us to experience the low points of life in order to teach us lessons that we could learn in no other way.

The past nine years have truly been an adventure. Not one that I would have wished, but an adventure just the same. I need only remind myself occasionally that it was an adventure of God's choosing.

All in all this has been one of many adventures of God's choosing. As I reach the end of this story, I cannot help but think of the beginning of my adventures with God, many years ago. It all began with a simple act of faith and trust.

Like everyone else, I was a sinner in need of far more than healing from a disease like Lyme. I needed forgiveness and redemption. I needed God's mercy to escape His judgment and I needed God's grace to gain eternal life with Him. That is only possible through Jesus Christ, the Son of God. His sacrificial death on a cross long ago granted the mercy and the pardon of my sins. His resurrection allowed the grace and the gift of life for all eternity in heaven for me, and for anyone who believes and places their faith in Him. The adventures of life since first trusting Him have merely been the preparation for the greatest adventure to come ... some day.

> *When a founder has cast a bell he does not presently fix it in the steeple, but tries it with his*

hammer, and beats it on every side to see if there be any flaw in it. So Christ doth not, presently after he has converted a man, convey him to heaven; but suffers him first to be beaten upon by many temptations, and then exalts him to his crown.

— RICHARD CECIL

About The Author

Dr. Paul Ashley has served as a pastor and has taught courses in Bible science, Bible history, and church history as well as Jewish culture, having been a student and teacher of the Text for over 30 years. He has been a frequent speaker on these subjects across the U.S.

He is also a distinguished internationally known scientist with over 35 years of service including Deputy Director of a research laboratory for missile development. He has authored over 200 publications and presentations as well as numerous patents. He is a graduate of Baylor University (1974) and Washington University (1978).

www.ingramcontent.com/pod-product-compliance
Lightning Source LLC
Chambersburg PA
CBHW021200020426
42331CB00003B/151